Family-Centered Intergenerational Religious Education

Director's Manual

Kathleen O. Chesto, D. Min.

Sheed & Ward

Imprimatur:
Most Reverend John F. Whealon
Archbishop of Hartford
August 15, 1988

Reverend Norman J. Belval, S.T.D.
Censor deputatus

Sheed & Ward™ is a service of National Catholic Reporter Publishing
Company, Inc.

ISBN: 1-55612-186-5

Published by: Sheed & Ward
               115 E. Armour Blvd. P.O. Box 419492
               Kansas City, MO 64141

To order, call: (800) 333-7373

Contents

1

The Spark:
An Introduction

The decade of the family is slowly drawing to a close. No one has commented on it; no one even refers to it any more. Everyone seems to be hoping that if we just ignore it, it will go away. We all tried the family programs and they just didn't work; or we knew they would never work in our parish so we didn't even try. "Parents are the primary educators" is no longer the good news of the '80's; it has become an ax to hold over the heads of parents who fail to participate in our programs or live up to our expectations.

The simple truth of the matter is that family religious education hasn't failed; it simply hasn't been tried. We have never actually attempted to put religion back into the family.

We put families into the classroom. We gave them textbooks and teachers, blackboards and grade-level divisions, and totally ignored the fact that families don't learn that way.

Much religious education is already happening in families; it simply has not been named. The parent who responds to a baby's cry has already taught that child the first and most important lesson on prayer: when you cry out at night, someone answers. The kindergartener who is lovingly prepared for the first day of school knows all about the God who prepares a way in the wilderness. It is up to religious educators to help families to name these religious experiences. As the USCC statement on family catechesis so beautifully puts it, "Family catechesis is the formalizing of the catechetical process already learned and continuously experienced in the family. (page 8)

If we are going to succeed in formalizing the process, we are going to need new models and new methods of religious education based on the way families normally function. Family learning is experiential. Families don't use textbooks and films to teach children how to walk. They hold the baby by the hands and let the little one experience walking. They provide an environment where it is safe for the child to experiment with taking steps. They encourage and praise, but for the most part, they wait patiently (unless it is their firstborn!) for the moment of readiness. Talking, eating, riding a bike, pumping a swing, are all taught in the same manner. For centuries, parents have been passing on life skills to their children. The traditions that have enriched life and made it sacred have been handed down in the wonderful stories of "remember when" shared on long winter evenings, around Christmas trees and campfires, at family reunions and other family "sacramental" moments.

Families not only suffer when we try to employ didactic methods of teaching, they are uncomfortable with grade level divisions. Families, like churches, are intergenerational by nature and function best in intergenerational groups. Everyone in a family is both teacher and learner, regardless of age. When a family goes swimming, they seldom divide into age groups. Each person is free to enjoy the water according to his/her ability. No one expects the baby to swim laps. Nor do they drain the pool for the one member who can't swim. All do everything they are capable of doing, with parents joining in the fun, offering occasional guidance, and learning new tricks themselves. In this situation, children learn to communicate with people of all ages, to give and receive respect, to affirm and to share. We are seeing family life at its very best when we are watching families relate intergenerationally.

Workable family catechesis is based on the family's intergenerational model, with people of all ages coming together to learn and to support one another, while enjoying each other's company. Family-Centered Intergenerational Religious Education is a program based on the family's own methods and models of functioning.. It attempts to establish small, intergenerational Christian communities where faith can be deepened, shared, and handed on within a strong support system for the Christian lifestyle.

Family-Centered Intergenerational Religious Education (FIRE) grew out of the needs of a particular parish, Sacred Heart Roman Catholic Church in Southbury, Connecticut. This is an affluent, middle class community of 1700 families in a rural setting that is quickly becoming suburban. The town and parish consist of three distinctly different groups of people: the farmers and townspeople who have lived in Southbury for generations; the retirement community of Heritage Village composed in large part of relocated New Yorkers; and the upper management people who presently represent more than half the population. These divisions and the transient nature of much of the population tend to exacerbate the isolationism of the age. The pastor who had come to the parish three years earlier had chosen as one of his primary tasks "creating a sense of community."

The loss of the director of religious education led to the evaluation of the entire process of religious formation in the parish. At a meeting attended by 121 parishioners, the people were divided into twelve groups and asked to prioritize their formational needs. They were given a list of possibilities to aid them, ranging from an adult lecture series to social youth ministry, and were asked to consider what they felt would be the most effective means of religious education for the parish. The number one priority in eleven of the twelve groups was family/intergenerational faith-sharing communities.

At this point in the process, the pastor requested my help. I had been meeting with a group of families in my own home who had been searching for a way to support one another and share their faith with their children. Everyone in our community was eager to share with the parish what we had experienced. I agreed to take on the task of developing a parish wide program based on the intergenerational model we had developed. FIRE (Family-centered Intergenerational Religious Education) grew out of that decision. It flows from that original community, my own personal convictions regarding religious education and the expressed need of the people of Sacred Heart Parish.

Eleven years have passed since that original group began meeting. The first families have become leaders of other groups. The idea has gone out to other parishes and dioceses, new families and new denominations adapting the program to their own needs and their own experience of God. The hope of all of us who formed that original core of families is that others will find what we have learned: that faith is not something you know, but something you do, and it is best passed on in the practice of faith-filled family living.

Goals

As an alternative model of religious education originally designed for the Roman Catholic Church, FIRE is based on the three basic elements given by the American bishops for all genuine catechesis: message, worship and service, done in the context of community.

> Catechetical ministry must be understood in relation to Jesus' threefold mission. It is a form of ministry of the word, which proclaims and teaches. It leads to and flows from the ministry of worship, which sanctifies through prayer and sacrament. It supports the ministry of service, which is linked to efforts to achieve social justice...[1]

The content of the program covers the main truths of the Catholic faith, as enumerated in the National Catechetical Directory, in a four-year cycle.

In an attempt to break away from the school model and to immerse families more deeply in the life of the church, each year is organized into liturgical segments with groups meeting during liturgical seasons and recessing during ordinary time. An Introductory Segment, designed to be done during Lent the year before the full program, acquaints people with the process of working in intergenerational groups.

As a liturgically oriented program with a catechetical basis, FIRE has seven specific goals.

1. To establish intergenerational communities where faith can be shared and values transmitted in an atmosphere of acceptance and support.

> If Christians are interested in preserving, expressing and deepening revelation, then their primary concern ought to be establishing communities that experience revelation.[2]

2. To encourage people to grow in their faith through prayer and Scripture study.

> The goal of religious education is persons who are continually growing and are able to respond openly to life and radically to Christ.[3]

3. To draw people more deeply into the liturgical life of the community.

> The liturgy is the summit toward which the activity of the church is directed; at the same time, it is the fountain from which all her power flows.[4]

4. To challenge people to live out the Christian message in service to others.

> "If good works do not go with it, faith is quite dead." (James 2:17)

5. To assist families:

> a) in developing communication and affirmation skills
>
> b) in talking about God and in praying together
>
> c) in discovering their gifts and using them in the service of others

> The family has received from God its mission to be the first and vital cell of society. It will fulfill its mission if it shows itself to be the domestic sanctuary of the Church through the mutual affection of its members

and the common prayer they offer to God, if the whole family is caught up in the liturgical worship of the church, and if it provides active hospitality and promotes justice and other good works for the service of all the brethren in need.[5]

6. To help people recognize the presence of God in their everyday lives and so internalize their concepts of faith and ministry.

All time and all flesh mediate the divine-human interaction.[6]

7. To teach people, especially children, that God is not boring and that learning about God can be fun.

Notes

1. United States Catholic Conference, *National Catechetical Directory.* (1979) #32.

2. Gabriel Moran. *The Present Revelation* (New York: Seabury, 1972) p. 299.

3. Sandra DeGidio. *Sharing Faith in the Family* (West Mystic, CT: Twenty-Third Publications, 1980) p. 8.

4. Vatican II, *The Constitution on the Sacred Liturgy,* 4 December 1963, #10

5. Vatican II, *Decree on the Apostolate of Lay People,* 18 November 1965, #11.

6. Moran. *op cit.* p. 268

2

Theoretical Foundations For Intergenerational Religious Education

The theoretical bases for this program are both educational and theological. While the structure and methodology of FIRE flow from a particular philosophy of learning, the idea itself is based on a specific theology of religious education.

Theology

"The Word became flesh and dwelt among us." (John 1:14)

God has become incarnate, able to be reached and touched and known, not only in Jesus, but in each one of us. With John, what we proclaim is "that which we have heard, and we have seen with our own eyes...that we have touched with our own hands..." (1 John 1:1). This is the mystery of the incarnation.

Therefore, to engage in religious education is no longer to transmit information about some distant deity in the hope that should people someday stumble across God, there would be recognition. It is rather to help people articulate their own experience, to discover those moments when the divine has broken through, become incarnate in their lives, and only then to help them to situate that experience within the greater faith story. H. Richard Niebuhr, in *Christ and Culture*, describes such a stance as "conversionist," finding Christ within culture, converting and transforming it. James Fenhagen, in *Mutual Ministry*, offers educators a schema for entering into that conversion process. His four major tasks of ministry—story-telling, community-building, symbol-sharing, and value-transmitting—form the structure within which FIRE's theology will be explained.

When Jesus appeared to the disciples on the road to Emmaus, he asked them to share their story. "What matters are you discussing as you walk along?" (Luke 24:17) It was only after bringing them in touch with their own reality that Jesus told them the larger story, helping them to see their story within the light of the full message of the prophets." (Luke 24:25)

One of the great failures of religious education is that we have told the story of a creating God before people experienced themselves as created, of a saving God before people experienced themselves as saved. Augustine tells us that "No one believes anything unless he first knows it to be believable." (de praedestatione sanctorum 2:5)

Understanding is not something a teacher has to offer simply by telling the story. As Peter Berger points out, "People move from their own human experiences to statements about God."[1] I would like to add the word "graced" experiences here in order to allow for God's action in the individual. Only after such experiences will the Christian story have an impact on one's lived reality.

In *Noise of Solemn Assemblies*, Berger insists that we are presently inoculating our youth with small doses of Christianoid concepts so that by the time they reach maturity they have been effectively immunized against any possibility of conversion. We give answers before there are questions, insuring the questions will never be explored. We have told our youth the story so many times devoid of their lived reality that they have become immune to being corrected or energized by it.

The problem is not new. In *The Prophetic Imagination*, Walter Brueggemann speaks of the same dilemma in Israel's history. Moses freed the Israelites from the oppressive government of pharoah only to have them establish the form of monarchy they had escaped. David sang of the crossing of the Reed Sea, of Jericho, and Gideon's victories while taking a census and counting the number of his soldiers. Solomon built a temple for the God who had descended in a cloud in the wilderness and who claimed to have no fixed dwelling.

We of the Roman Catholic church preached a "just war" theory while promoting a Jesus who said "Offer no defense."

(Matthew 5:39) It was not that we had stopped telling the story; we had stopped holding the present up against the story to be convicted and corrected by it. "Fidelity does not consist in conserving or merely repeating the past, but rather in unlocking and releasing it. For only human being have the ability to review the past in order to correct the mistakes of the present."[2] If religious education is to help us to claim our story in such a dynamic and life-giving fashion, it will need tools. In *Models of Revelation*, Avery Dulles suggests that symbols are the tools we use in order to mediate our story with the greater faith story. The religious educator must mine the memory of the people and discover the symbols in everyday life that can be signs of hope and contact with a greater reality. This is what Ghandi did for his people with salt and cloth. He imbued the symbols of their oppression with the hope of freedom. This is what Jesus did with the messianic banquet and the common elements of bread and wine.

The following is a simple story from my own life in which I, as an educator, use symbol to perform that mediating function.

> My mom made the best pancakes in the whole world; at least, growing up, I always believed she did. There was a whole ritual that went with pancakes in our house. We would arrive in the kitchen in the morning to find it filled with the aroma and Mom busy at the stove. She served each of us individually. As she placed the plate of steaming flapjacks in front of each child she would say,
>
> "Your mother makes the best pancakes in the whole world."
>
> When she finally sat down with her own breakfast, we would all say in unison,

"Our mother makes the best pancakes in the whole world."

When I would visit friends and be served pancakes, I would respond by telling them that my mother made the best pancakes in the whole world. It did little to endear me to their mothers.

As I grew older, I discovered that other people made excellent pancakes, some even better than my Mom's. It took years before I finally had the courage to suggest this to her. When I did mention that perhaps other people's pancakes were as good as hers, she simply smiled and said, 'I know.'

"Then why," I asked, "have you been telling me all these years that my mother makes the best pancakes in the whole world?"

She responded with a question,

'What do you think of every time you eat pancakes?'

"I think of you."

"As long as there are pancakes, you'll remember me."

And Jesus said: "Whenever you eat this bread or drink this cup, do it to remember me."

It is my own story, my personal history, but the symbolism lifts it out of the personal realm and situates it firmly in the middle of the Jesus story. Because it deals with the simple facts of ordinary life, others can see in it, not only the Jesus story, but their own story as well.

Symbols, in mediating our stories and revitalizing our beliefs, celebrate realities in our lives that defy words and explanations. Symbols put us in touch with the transcendent in life. As people come to a greater awareness of the symbolic, there is a greater appreciation and participation in ritual. Religious education, if it is to call people to a fuller experience of their own reality in the light of the faith story, must overflow into ritualized prayer and worship.

In worship, as in story, it is important for symbols to be true not only to our present but to incorporate our past, while reminding us that we are the people who "wait in joyful hope for the coming of our Savior Jesus Christ."[3]

As the bishops at Medellin pointed out, our symbols and liturgical signs should be expressive not only of what has been accomplished in the church's journey toward eschatalogical fulfillment, but also in measuring what is lacking to reach it. The community that celebrates true liturgy will find that not only is their worship shaped by their lived reality, but that reality is, in turn, shaped by their prayer.

If community is, then, the normal context for sharing symbol and story (as I have implied above) must we "build community" before we can engage in truly effective religious education?

I do not believe that communities are built, despite the work of Fenhagen and others who claim that "community building" is one of the main tasks of the minister. Communities grow, usually out of the sharing of symbol and story. Community happened among the three on the road to Emmaus in the sharing of the story and the breaking of the bread. Community happened among the half-million on the road to the United Nations, telling their story in the one-line song, "All we are saying is give peace a chance." Community happened on Ghandi's march to the sea and on the Mayan Indians' march to Guatemala City. No one indulged in T-group training or Serendipity exercises. People were bound together by an overwhelming present reality and the hope for a better future.

There are, within our churches today, people crying out against the isolationism and the injustices of this age, fearful of a future clouded by the threat of nuclear destruction and overwhelmed by the task of handing on values and beliefs in an almost valueless society. It is our task, as religious educators, to call people together, providing a structure where faith can be experienced and shared and where people can be challenged and supported in making their faith inform and transform their lives. In such a context, community will grow. Others will be attracted to that community and will, in turn, experience faith.

Among those in need of community in our churches are our children. While the life experiences of children may be limited, their experiences of God have a great deal to teach all of us. Paul VI in his decree "On Evangelization" insisted that children proclaim the gospel by their very lives. Jesus instructed us all to become like little children. In reflecting on this truth, John Westerhoff insists:

> We cannot afford to accept the separation of children, youth and adults...The needs of various persons may differ, but we grow only when we share our differences in community. Peer group isolation prevents growth.[4]

When we isolate our children in the name of religious education, religion and education, adults and children, all suffer.

The Word made flesh dwells in each of us, regardless of age. Jesus became a child in our midst to lead us to God. Incarnation invites us to call the children into our midst that together we might journey to God.

This is the general theological foundation on which the program is built. It flows from an incarnational perspective and calls upon its leaders to be story-tellers and symbol sharers, its communities to be value transmitters. Each of the four years within the program has a specific theological theme at its heart. *Year I: God Speaks* explores the idea of revelation. Our God is a God who communicates, through history, through the prophets, in the Word spoken in Jesus, in the Spirit who continues to speak in the world today. "By this revelation then, the deepest truth about God and the salvation of man is made clear to us in Christ who is the Mediator and at the same time the fullness of all revelation. God, who through the Word creates all things and keeps them in existence, gives men an enduring witness to Himself in created realities." (Vatican II Divine Revelation #2,3)

Within the year, each liturgical segment (Advent, Lent, Easter) and each lesson within a segment is based on a particular theological perspective. The Advent Segment is based largely on Walter Brueggemann's concept of prophecy in Israel, backed by Gerhard Von Rad's theology of prophetic calling. Both Brueggemann and Von Rad insist that Israel's prophets were not "seers" but "readers," individuals who read the signs of the times and were not afraid to proclaim the reality they saw. While both men recognize Moses as the first of the prophets, they see prophecy as most intimately connected to the rise and fall of the kingdom.

Brueggemann divides the prophets into two categories: those called to "tell it like it is," and those called to "tell it like it could be." The first were the prophets of the kingdom period, a time he sees as closely related to our world today. These prophets challenged the corruption of Israel's political leaders and her religious practices while warning of the destruction that such corruption could bring. The second group of prophets were from the captivity and post-captivity periods. Their task was to comfort the people and give them hope.

Within this context, a lesson on prophecy examines the prophetic call given to all Christians in Baptism and alerts participants to those signs of the times we may be asked to address within our own particular communities. Jeremiah and Ezechiel, prophets called to "tell it like it is," provide an opportunity to look at the reality of sin and reconciliation. Isaiah, called to "tell it like it could be," is the basis for our study of Messiah, and later in the year, for our study of the Kingdom.

The Lenten Segment of Year I is based largely on the implicit Christology of Raymond Brown in *Jesus: God and Man* and on the pontifical biblical statement on "The Historical Truth of the Gospels." This theological perspective insists that Jesus grew in his understanding of his role as Messiah. The Gospels, as post-resurrectional accounts, offer a faith perspective of Jesus, rather than an historical account of his ministry. Even within the Gospels themselves, a growth in Christology is evident from Mark to John.

With this in mind, the Lenten Segment begins with the humanity of Jesus and attempts to discover how he might have appeared to the people of his day. The lessons move through discipleship and prayer to redemption and only then to resurrection and divinity. The Eucharist lesson focuses on the concept of a "remembering meal." Our Eucharistic prayer recalls Jesus' invitation "Do this in memory of me." Regis Duffy in *Real Presence* reminds us of the commitment in remembering. "Disappointed disciples, after recognizing Jesus in the breaking of the bread at Emmaus, say to one another. "'Were not our hearts burning inside us as he talked to us on the road and explained the Scriptures to us?' They got up immediately and returned to Jerusalem..." (Luke 24:32-33). There they witness to a Risen Lord. Jesus himself prepares an early morning meal for his dispirited disciples by the shore of the Sea of Tiberias and then commissions a repentant Peter to "Feed my sheep (John 21:17)." (p. 137)

The Easter Segment follows the Lucan timetable for the gift of the Spirit. In accord with Thomas Aquinas (*Summa Theologica*, Ia IIae, QQ 68-70) the Spirit is described as being known only through its attributes and fruits (Galatians 5:22-

23). Aquinas calls these attributes virtues and defines them as "meritorious" only when they lead to right action. The actions to which the fruits of the Spirit lead are beatitudes. In keeping with the Aquinas sequence, we began with the Pentecost story (Acts 2), moved to the "proofs" of the presence of the Spirit, and ended with the beatitudes (Matthew 5:1-12) as the actions of a Spirit-filled community. The lengthy argument of Aquinas on the nature and essence of the Spirit was not addressed. We spoke of the Spirit simply as the way in which God continues to communicate and to be present to us today.

Year II: We Respond in Sign and Symbol explores sacraments as the way in which we respond to the God who loved us first. Symbols and rituals as they occur naturally in the family are explored first, the families are encouraged to developed a sense of ritual. The Church is discussed as the primary sacrament (Lumen Gentium) with all other sacramental actions flowing from it. Sacraments are presented as the way in which we become present to the God who is always present to us. The year is rich in family ritual, with strong encouragement to participate in parish ritual.

Year III: God's Voice in History, uses simulation games, storytelling, and drama to help families identify with our Hebrew ancestors. The glorified Bible-story methodology is avoided: Families are encouraged through the history of Roland DeVaux and the explanations of Bernhard Anderson to view both patriarchs and matriarchs as real people, to read what *Numbers* really says about the sojourn in the desert, and to consider the rise and fall of the kingdom in an historical as well as faith perspective. The meaning of these events for today is explored through the *Peace Pastoral* and the *Pastoral on the Economy*.

Year IV: We Believe basically tries to include any elements that may have been missed in the three years. The role of Mary, the Church and the saints is stressed. Jesus is central to the year, his life in the holy family, his ministry in Israel, his ongoing presence with the church. Underlying the entire year is the question "What distinguishes us as Christians?" "What distinguishes us as Roman Catholics, or as any given denomination?" "How do I believe and how do I live what makes me different from a non- believer?"

Throughout the program, the community is called to do theology and to live by theological values. The hope of the process is not that they will come to recognize the Christology of Brown, but that they will come to see the Christ present and acting in their own lives. It is in the service of this hope that the following philosophy of education and its distinct methodology were developed.

Philosophy of Education

In one of his earlier books, *Creative Ministry*, Henri Nouwen distinguishes between violent and non-violent learning. The first he sees as deductive and competitive, imposing knowledge on passive receivers regardless of their need or desire for that knowledge or respect for the knowledge they may already possess. It is a consumer based educational philosophy, dependent on the acquisition of facts, with little emphasis on the internalization of information or the formation of the student. John Holt, in *How Children Fail*, described this imposition of knowledge as the principal reason for student failure in school. The great educator Benjamin Bloom, in *Taxonomy of Educational Objectives*, calls this educational process a structural flaw so serious as to necessitate the rehabilitation of the whole system. In this teacher-centered learning, the success of one student depends on the failure of another, since this is the method by which class rank, college admission, etc. will be determined. Knowledge becomes property to be guarded, rather than gift to be shared. As Nouwen points out, it is disrespectful, destructive, and competitive. It has been, however, the principal method used in Catholic religious education since the Council of Trent. It is the method employed by the catechisms and the various texts promoted since the Second Vatican Council.

Non-violent or redemptive learning, as Nouwen calls it, views education as a process of "leading out," as the derivation of the word *education* implies (from *educare:* to lead out). The teacher is a companion on a journey with the student; "each tries to evoke in the other (their) respective potentials and make them available to each other."[5] It is an inductive process, beginning in the experience of the individual and leading to knowledge which is more readily internalized precisely because it flows from real experience. The focus is no longer on knowing the answers to a set of preconceived questions, but on discovering what one's own religious questions are.

For Gabriel Moran, understanding one's own religious question is the basis of all religious education. Religion itself is not based first in the testimony of an ancient prophet conveyed to us through what he calls questionable documents, but rather, "in the experience of each person who opens himself/ (herself) to the possibility of the divine and joins with other (persons) in examining the human and the divine in revelation."[6]

The importance of giving each person time to discover one's own questions before presenting preconceived answers was brought home to me graphically by my son at age seven.

Purely out of curiosity, I had decided to give him the eighth grade religion test. One of the True/False statements read: "God revealed himself fully in creation." Students were expected to answer "False" and to list the means of revelation they had been taught in class. Some even managed to do this. Jonathan read the question and answered "True" without a moment of hesitation.

"But, Jon," I protested, "You know that God was revealed in the prophets and in Jesus and..."

"Mommy," he interrupted, "It doesn't say God revealed himself 'only.' It says God revealed himself 'fully.' I think he did. Then he had to send all those other things because we didn't hear what he said the first time."

Because he did not have available to him the expected answer, he was able to ask his own question, "Since everything on earth shouts out God's name, why did God continue to speak?" It was a natural question for a child whose experience was one of a deep reverence for nature. His answer, borne out by Jesus in the parable of the tenants (Matthew 21:33-42), is an accurate summation of Moran's theology of revelation that sees every divine act as totally revelational and limited only by our perception. The reply also demonstrates an initial understanding of the concept of sin. The whole thought process was possible only because Jonathan had never been given the "right" answer.

Thomas Groome, in *Christian Religious Education*, also stresses that all religious education begins in the experience of the individual and the religious questions that life has posed to the person. Groome has developed a specific five-step method for reflection and education that has become the framework for many of the texts being published within the Catholic Church today. In Groome's method, persons are called: a. to examine the life experience underlying the theme of the lesson; b. to reflect together upon the experience and its implications for the theological theme; c. to consult the story of faith on the particular theme; d. to recall what they have learned about faith and how that could impact on their living; e. to respond to Jesus.

While I agree with Groome's theory, his method does not work for an intergenerational group. He begins by inviting people to reflect on experiences they have already had and moves from this point to discussion. Children of various ages may not have had the experience necessary to be able to reflect on the theological principle Groome hopes to explore. We have found, in dealing with a group where the ages vary widely, education works best when people can actually participate in the experience together.

FIRE's method is much like that used in an experiential science class. An "experiment," or experience, is structured in such a way that it will give rise to the questions the "class" hopes to address. It is completely inductive, beginning in a simulated life experience and leading to reflection on the theological principles involved. The way in which this is accomplished can be best understood through describing a typical FIRE lesson.

The very first experience shared by individuals or families coming to FIRE is called **STORYTELLING.** The point of this particular session is to introduce the manner in which the Scriptures were written. When Roman Catholics began reading the Bible after Vatican II, they fell easily into the trap of literalism. Since FIRE is based almost entirely on Scripture, it is necessary to examine the whole idea of truth in the Scriptures.

We came together for this session one month after the hostages were released from Iran. Taking that news event, and dividing the community into four groups, we asked each group to tell the story of the release. They were required to relate the facts with as much historical accuracy as possible. After they had moved into groups, the leader went around and quietly told each group their particular perspective: one group was writing for an Iranian college newspaper; one group was writing for the New York Times; one group was telling the story to a first grade class; one group was a hostage writing a letter home. They were all instructed not to reveal to the other groups their particular editorial perspective.

When the groups came together and heard each other's stories, everyone had great fun guessing the perspective of each account. It was easy to see that while everyone had told the truth, the editorial bias had produced entirely different stories. The question arose naturally: What affects the way a story is written? Drawing from the experience they had just shared, they were able to give the four factors Von Rad lists in his *Theology of the Old Testament* as being the principal influences on the way in scripture was written: who is reporting, why, to whom, and with what tradition they are aligning themselves. Later, when participants were confronted with conflicting accounts of the same event in Scripture, they were not threatened, but were able to consider the factors that might have caused these differences.

Actually participating in an experience and uncovering its underlying theological perspective enables individuals to recognize more readily the way God intervenes in the everydayness of their lives. A "family reunion" that leads to a reflection on Eucharist helps people to see the Eucharist element in every family meal. A "changing country" experience that leads to a reflection on resurrection enables people to consider the "letting go" experiences in everyday life as part of the death-resurrection cycle.

Not only do experiences offer people the opportunity to reflect theologically on life, they offer the possibility of prayer. If the purpose of religious education is to bring us to the love and knowledge of God, then all education should lead to communion with the Divine. It is not possible to give people an experience of God; it is possible, however, to structure into an experience the silence and space that make prayer possible.

Creating inductive experiences based on everyday life to teach theological principles is a time consuming and difficult task. Yet, I believe it to be a far more effective and respectful form of religious education. It is also the only method I have found to work in an intergenerational setting. It allows each person to grasp as much of the experience as they are ready and able to understand. It offers adults the opportunity to learn from the wisdom and simplicity of children while giving children the opportunity to share the feelings and faith of the adults. I have heard a five-year-old speak of starting school as a death experience and a forty-five-year-old recognize her spouse's death as a resurrection all in the same lesson.

The Word became flesh. FIRE attempts, both theologically and philosophically, to find that Word enfleshed in people's lives and to offer a community in which that Word can be experienced and known.

Before this can happen, parents need to believe that it is possible, that they are capable of handing on faith to their children in a Church that has traditionally retained that right for its religious ministers. "Parents are the primary educators" must cease to be a club brandished over parents' heads to insure their attendance at meetings. This truth must be understood as the Good News that it is, a proclamation of an already existing reality.

In an effort to educate members of Sacred Heart Parish to this understanding of religious education, I gave the following talk entitled "Family Spirituality" to launch the FIRE program. It is now available in Video from FIRE Productions, PO Box 1016, Southbury, CT 06488.

Family Spirituality

Do you remember the story of the rich young man who came to Jesus asking what he must do to be saved? He had kept the commandments from his youth, and Mark tells us that Jesus looked on him and loved him. Then he told him: "There is one more thing you must do. Go and sell what you have and give to the poor...and come, follow me." (Mark 10:21)

Who are the people that sell what they have and give to the poor in order to follow the Lord? I grew up in the Roman Catholic tradition and I was always taught that the ones who left everything to follow the Lord were the nuns and priests. Marriage was always a kind of second rate choice, what you did if you were unable to follow the higher "path."

Paul started it all when he said that he wished we could all be celibate like he was, but that it was better to be married than burn. Not exactly a rousing endorsement for marriage as a way to achieve sanctity! The Church argued for centuries over whether or not people who were sexually intimate could pray. Council after Council discussed the issue until they concluded, in true Church style, that of course married people could pray, but they could pray better if they abstained from sex.[7]

Each of us who grew up within this tradition carries this history somewhere within us. Somewhere along the way, we were taught to see ourselves as not quite holy, not quite good, not quite willing to sacrifice all for the sake of the kingdom.

I am here tonight to tell you that it's not true! We have been cheated out of our heritage. I wonder how many of you did, in fact, give up everything, wipe out little savings accounts, given all you had to start a new community called a family? How many of you stopped spending anything on yourselves in order to pay a mortgage to house that new community? How many of you gave up a nice little sports car for the station wagon that would carry the plywood to finish the family room, while leaving space for the kids?

We, too, gave up what we had to follow the Lord. We, too, are called to holiness and to service in the kingdom. The only difference is that we are called in partnership.

One of the first ministries that most of us experienced was service to the children that God sent into our lives. We began, at the moment of birth, to teach our children about the Lord. Now, I suspect some of you doubt that you really did that, but I know you did. There isn't a parent here who has not picked up a crying baby. If you have done that, then you have taught the first, the most important lesson on prayer: when you cry out at night, someone answers. Without that knowledge, that faith, it is impossible to pray.

When your little one was about six months old you all started that marvelous game of peek-a-boo. Gradually, your baby learned that you were present, even when you couldn't be seen. If all reality is not always visible, it becomes possible to believe in an invisible God.

You celebrated sacraments daily with your children as toddlers. While they played, blissfully unaware of your presence, you were always aware of them and called them to you for a story, a meal, to kiss away their hurts. And so they came to believe in a God who was always present to them, even when they were unaware of that Presence. It became possible for them to understand that stories and meals and healing were ways to come in touch with the Divine Presence in their lives.

I wonder how many of you have prepared a child for the first day at school. I remember getting our first child ready for this experience. We visited the school and met the teacher, we drove the bus route, took walks to the bus stop, and bought new clothes, shoes, and a new lunch box. The night before, when the clothes were laid out, the bath and story finished, and my five-year-old was in bed, I sat at the kitchen table. In my mind, I tried to picture his day, to see if I had forgotten anything. I saw him climb up the steps of the bus, find a seat, and open his lunch box to check on his meal. Then I saw his milk money fall to the floor! I jumped up quickly and taped it to the inside of the lunch box. I know you have done the same. A child who has experienced that kind of care has already received the best possible lesson on the providence of God, a God who goes before and prepares the way for us. All that is left for religious education to do is to give that experience its theological name.

This teaching, though, has not been all one-sided. I used to think that God gave me children so that I could raise them as Christians. It was a great and awesome task. I am not so sure anymore that was God's purpose. Let me share with you a story to explain.

> It was the era of the lawn in our marriage. You know, the time when you own your first home and nothing is quite as important as THE LAWN. And so you cut and water and weed and fertilize so that you can cut some more. It usually takes a summer to realize that crabgrass is also green and will do just fine.

We were in the particular phase of the era known as the war on the dandelions. My husband was busy digging up all the roots when my three-year-old son appeared at the back door. His hands were filled with the wilted blossoms and tears were steaming down his face.

"Mommy! Daddy is digging up all the flowers!"

"Those aren't flowers," I responded, much too quickly. "Those are weeds."

"Why?" he asked, in typical three-year-old fashion.

Why indeed? Since I had no idea, I did what every good mother would do in that situation. I told him to go outside and play and I would think about it and call him when I had an answer.

I did think about it seriously. Why were the dandelions weeds? They looked just like the marigolds we were planting all along the walk. Why had I given my son such a confusing idea?

Soon, I felt a small presence beside me. I looked down into huge, accusing brown eyes as my son said:

"I know why the dandelions are weeds, Mommy."

Since I still didn't know, I asked him,

"Why, Jon?"

"It's because they don't grow where *you* want them to."

Which is precisely why the dandelions are weeds!

Where had my child acquired such wisdom? I began to suspect that God had not given me children to raise them as Christians. God had given me children to raise me as Christian. That was the day I started really listening to the things my children said. Their theology was beautiful.

I remember coming across Elizabeth at two years of age, celebrating Eucharist in her room with a brass candlestick and a small white disk. Over and over again she repeated, "This is my Body." When I asked her later if she had hoped to change the disk into Jesus, she responded, "Oh no. I change Wizbef into Jesus." It only took a moment to realize how much better her theology was than mine. What does it matter if the bread and wine are changed if the people who celebrate with bread and wine are not transformed into Jesus? Six graduate credits in sacramental theology had failed to teach me what my child had grasped at two.

We have always had the custom of celebrating Advent with a little prayer service each night. The children took turns choosing a "Jesus" song for our celebration. On this particular night, it was Becky's turn to choose. She was five, at the time, and she chose "Rudolph, The Red-nosed Reindeer" as her song. I explained patiently that it was not a Jesus song. She was probably confused because we sang it at Christmas. She insisted it was indeed a Jesus song, but could not explain what she meant. As her eyes filled with tears, my husband pointed out that I was being foolish and it just didn't matter. Anything can be prayer and of course we would sing it.

Have you ever listened, really listened, to the words to Rudolph? How he was an outcast and was laughed at and excluded? Sounds a lot like the Suffering Servant songs of Isaiah. And how did he come to us? As a light, on Christmas Eve, bringing us gifts. As we finished singing, I turned excitedly to Becky.

"You meant that Jesus suffered, too, and that he comes as a light on Christmas!"

"Yes, Mommy!" she responded, delighted that I had finally overcome my stupidity.

I could give you countless examples of the ways my children have taught me about God, but you, too, have those stories and those experiences. God gave us children so that we could become Christian. God knew we would have a hard time without them. We give them our values and hand on our faith, but in the end, we leave them free to choose for themselves. If they choose other than what we have taught them, that does not make us bad parents. We are good parents if *we* become beautiful through the process of parenting. What our children become is their free choice.

(A few moments of silence)

I have a vision. It is of all of us standing before the Lord on judgement day. And the Lord will say: "I was hungry, and you fed me, thirsty, and you gave me a drink, naked and you clothed me, homeless and you sheltered me, imprisoned and you visited me..." (Matthew 25:36)

Puzzled, we'll respond:

"When, Lord, when did I see you hungry?"

And the Lord will say:

"How could you ask? You of the three and a half million peanut butter and jelly sandwiches, how could you even ask?"

"But thirsty, Lord?"

"I was in the Kool-Ade line that came in with the summer heat and the flies and left mud on your floor and fingerprints on your walls and you gave me a drink."

"Naked, Lord, homeless?"

"I was born to you naked and homeless and you sheltered me, first in wombs and then in arms, and clothed me with your love. And you spent the next twenty years keeping me in jeans."

"But imprisoned, Lord? I know I didn't visit you in prison. I was never in a prison."

"Oh yes, for I was imprisoned in my littleness, behind the bars of a crib and I cried out in the night and you came. I was imprisoned inside an eleven-year-old body that was bursting with so many new emotions I didn't know who I was and you loved me into being myself. And I was imprisoned behind my teenage rebellion, my anger, and my stereo set, and you waited outside my locked door for me to let you in.

"Now, beloved, enter into the joy which has been prepared for you from all eternity."

Amen

For every parent who believes this, FIRE is possible.

Notes

1. Peter Berger. *Rumor of Angels* (Garden City, N.Y.: Doubleday, 1969) p. 60.

2. Rafael Avila. *Worship and Politics* (New York: Orbis, 1981) p. 3.

3. "Eucharist Prayer II," *Roman Catholic Canon.*

4. John H. Westerhoff III and Gwen Kennedy Neville. *Learning Through Liturgy* (New York: Seabury, 1978) p. 103.

5. Herri Nouwen. *Creative Ministry* (New York: Doubleday, 1978) p. 12.

6. Gabriel Moran. *The Present Revelation* (New York: Seabury Press: 1972) p. 180.

7. Joseph E. Kerns. *The Theology of Marriage* (New York: Sheed and Ward, 1964) Chapter 5.

3

Essential Components of an Intergenerational Program

The FIRE program changed continually during its five year evolution, reflecting the on-going evaluation and changing needs of the participants. However, certain basic components emerged as essential to the success of the program in any church: the planning committee, home groups, leadership, background sessions, and the large group activities. Each is explained here in detail and a time line demonstrates the position that each of these components occupied in the program. Also included in this chapter is a sample home group lesson, in order to demonstrate in detail how the lessons were carried out.

I would like to issue a word of caution. FIRE grew out of the needs of a specific community at a particular moment in time. Anyone intending to use the program in another setting should remain attentive to the needs of that community, adapting the process by prayerfully responding to the people at hand. While I have outlined a very specific program, it should be used more as a list of ingredients than as a recipe, more as a compass than a map. It is a grass roots program and works best when it grows out of the desires of the people within a community.

Planning Committee

The planning committee was the group of people responsible for designing and writing the FIRE program. It met weekly for three hours throughout the four-and-a-half years it took to design the entire process.

When I originally asked for people to assist in putting together the experiences for FIRE, no one responded. It took a personal invitation and some persuading to convince people that they were capable of performing the task. The original planning group consisted of one mother of preschoolers, two mothers of grade-school children, one mother of teenagers, a single person and myself. Because the group met during the morning on weekdays, it limited the participation of those who worked full time. While the original members remained the same, the group often expanded to include fathers or mothers on vacation, people within the FIRE program who simply wanted a taste of how the lessons were put together, and people who had only a limited stretch of time to give. The core who remained throughout became my support group and advisory committee.

The group gathered on Wednesday mornings at my home. We always began with a short time to socialize, talk about children or jobs, and share a cup of tea or coffee. The next forty-five minutes were spent in shared prayer. We would frequently begin with the scripture that was going to be the basis of our lesson and explore the ways God was speaking to each of us in the passage. This was also a special time of prayer for the people who were in FIRE, the communities and their leaders, the entire parish, and the world at large. I am convinced that the program had the impact that it did because of this ongoing commitment to prayer.

At the close of our prayer, I would discuss with the group the theology behind the topic we were addressing. During Year I, this frequently meant explanations of redaction criticism, brief summaries of various commentaries on a text, as well as a clear statement on our own church's position.

At this point, we would consider two questions. What questions did we want the group to raise around this topic (since we were committed to answering only those questions that arose from the group)? How did we experience this belief in everyday life?

When we did the experience on prophecy (Advent Segment II), we hoped to raise three questions:

What is a prophet?

What does it feel like to be "called"?

Am I willing to respond to God's call?

We decided that we experienced what it meant to be prophet when we were asked to take a stand on some of the current social justice issues in town. Important issues at that time were zoning, alcohol abuse, and vandalism. Using those issues, we created an imaginary scenario in which all of us were asked to take a stand on an issue appropriate to our ages. We discussed possible feelings and reactions and how these could be handled effectively by the leaders. Then we looked for scripture passages showing the reluctant responses of Israel's prophets.

The key word in this process is "imaginary." We found that in creating imaginary situations, people were freer to express their real feelings because it "didn't count." At the same time, the situations had to be lifelike, or there would be no carry-over into everyday life.

The creation of a realistic experience frequently involved three or four meetings. In the process, we would look at whether or not it would succeed in involving people of all ages, each of us sharing how our own particular children would respond. If it involved families working together as a unit, we would discuss the ways to involve the singles in the group.

The next step was to consider what part of the experience we wanted brought home. In the prophecy lesson, we wanted everyone to look at the opportunities to be prophet that the "signs of the times" might be presenting to them during the week. For many, the idea of a prophet being one who spoke out against the visible ills in society, rather than one who told the future, was a new idea. We wanted people to examine that idea in the life of one of the prophets. We suggested that any Take Homes (suggestion sheets for home activities) be done as dinner table discussions.

The last step was to plan a closing prayer celebration for the session. Here we relied heavily on symbols, silence and music in order for the prayer to appeal to the various ages present. The prayer time usually contained an affirmation or celebration of what had just been experienced. In the prophecy lesson, we gave everyone a chance to respond positively to God's call, then presented them with symbols of that calling. We had planned on using candles, but our mother of preschoolers pointed out the danger involved. In the end, heads of households received the candle while everyone else received a small packet of salt and the admonition to live as "salt of the earth."

When the lesson was finished, it was my task to write it up and present it at the next meeting. The entire process could take from three to six weeks. It was certainly not the most efficient way to plan a program, yet the planning committee remained the heart of FIRE.

Now that the program is available in finished form, churches may feel that this particular aspect of the program in unnecessary. However, I feel it is still important to have a core group who reviews the lessons and modifies them to fit the needs of the community.

Far more important is having a group that prays regularly for the people involved in the program. There is a Hebrew tradition from intertestamental times that speaks of a *zaddiq*, a person who was believed to be essential to the salvation of humankind. All mercy and goodness were channeled through this person. An earlier tradition saw this not as one person, but as thirty people. They were not necessarily known or respected. They were more apt to be the *anawim*, the poor, without power or wealth or status. It was their prayer life, though, that was responsible for grace in the world. The planning committee was the *zaddiq* for FIRE.

Home Groups

The home group was the basic unit of FIRE. We began with nine groups for a total of forty households in our Introductory Segment and grew to eleven groups and seventy-two households at the beginning of our first full year. Most groups were composed of five to seven households for a total of eighteen to thirty members per group. We found that fewer than four families in a group meant that it was difficult to do a lesson if one family was missing. Most of the experiences involved subdividing into three or more smaller groups. This is difficult with fewer than eighteen people, especially when you consider that some of the members might be quite young.

The groups met in homes and the size of the homes also had a bearing on the size of the groups. We found that an average raised ranch, the most typical home involved, will accommodate twenty-five people if half of them are children. A home that allows separate places for groups to discuss (e.g. family room, living room, kitchen) is ideal, but not really essential. A home provides the atmosphere in which families normally function and is, for this reason, a more comfortable learning environment. Even if our church had had the facilities to accommodate the groups (it did not), we would still have chosen to meet in homes.

There were two disadvantages to this. Equipment and materials had to be transported, and two groups could not use audio visual materials on the same night. The groups were also isolated from one another. The first problem we simply worked around. The second we solved with large group gatherings described later in this chapter.

The home groups met five times during the Introductory Segment. During this segment, the commitment level was poor. Evaluation by leaders at the end of this section revealed that a large part of this problem was due to the fact that FIRE was seen as an extra, a supplement, to the "regular" program. Therefore, it was not really important to attend.

The decision was made to ask families to choose between FIRE and the grade-level program for Year I. This placed greater emphasis on the program as an alternative form of religious education. The Covenant Meeting was also introduced. Each group was asked to write a contract with one another, agreeing to some of the basic requirements for functioning as a community. This process is explained fully in the Leader's Notes in the Leader's Manual for the Introductory Segment to the program. These "covenants" were signed and blessed in a large group celebration at the beginning of Year I.

During Year I, families met in home groups sixteen times. Attendance that year was excellent, with only three families out of seventy-two missing more than two meetings, and the vast majority missing none.

A typical home group meeting lasted one to two hours. The lessons themselves are designed to be completed in forty-five to sixty minutes. Some groups served refreshments; some groups spent more time socializing before the meeting. Groups with several small children moved through the lessons more quickly. The average length of a meeting was ninety minutes. This allowed time for the lesson and refreshments. Since one of the primary goals of the program was to create community, groups were encouraged to set a leisurely pace with space for sharing.

Meeting dates, times and places were agreed upon by the individual communities. The leader's meetings provided a rough structure, since two home sessions needed to be completed between each meeting. Large group sessions also provided some structure, with one at the beginning and end of each segment. Nine of the eleven groups added parties, pot luck suppers, and picnics to their regular schedule of meetings.

There are many factors that could be considered in putting a home group together. I found the most important were matching children, so that each child had someone to relate to, offering single parent families the "missing parent" model as well as another single parent family for companionship, and giving as many communities as possible a single adult. It is helpful not to have too many pre- schoolers in one group, but in our case, the young families were already friends and chose to be together.

We had 276 people in home groups, ranging in age from three months to seventy-eight years. Particular activities were occasionally planned for the very young, but, for the most part, they wandered in and out of the groups, joining in the singing and celebrating, tasting rather than understanding community.

We did not introduce new people to the groups at any point during the year. We asked new families wishing to join to wait until the following year. At that time, they were either placed in groups that had room or organized into new groups.

Seven of the eleven groups became tight knit communities that remained together for several years. Two fell apart and their members left or joined other groups. Two remained rather loosely bound together, more like a home class than a community.

Several factors determined whether a group became a community. The commitment of the individuals involved had a tremendous impact. It only took one family continually absenting itself and saying by its absence, "You are not important to us," to shake a budding sense of belonging. Human factors such as personality differences played a role. But the most important factor in determining whether or not a group became a community was the element we will consider next: LEADERSHIP.

Leadership

Experience has proven that leaders and their training are the most crucial element in FIRE. Basically, "leadership is the execution of a particular kind of role within an organized group, and essentially this role is defined...in terms of the ability to influence others."[1] Margaret Sawin, founder of the family cluster model and author of two books on the subject, gives three types of leadership possible in family/inter-generational clusters:

1. Rotating leadership
   among various individuals in the group
   among families in the group

2. Assigned leadership
   to an individual chosen by the group's participants
   to a family unit chosen by the group's participants
   to an individual chosen by the sponsoring organization

3. No assigned leadership

When we began the FIRE program, it was with leadership assigned by the sponsoring organization. This offered us the opportunity to prepare leaders more thoroughly, particularly in theology and group dynamics. It offered the groups a sense of stability and authorization. We found this to be an extremely important point in the beginning, perhaps because our church is so authoritative. As families remained in FIRE, they became better able to choose their own leaders and invest group authority in them without the church's direct intervention.

Assigned leadership also gave the leaders the opportunity to grow into a strong support community for each other which proved essential during our first two years. In a rotating leadership situation, this would not have been possible. Eventually, leaders found their support within their home group communities.

At the outset, leadership was invested primarily in adults. As the communities grew stronger and leaders more secure, families took on greater responsibility for directing the group.

There were disadvantages to assigned leadership. It took the group members longer to develop a sense of ownership of the group. We found they were inclined to call the group by the leader's name, e.g. "I am in Chesto's group," further divorcing themselves from power and control. To alleviate some of this problem, we asked the groups to choose a name for their cluster. This did much to develop a sense of group identity, and in a short time people referred to themselves as belonging to "the Voyagers," "the Rainbow Connection," etc.

Another disadvantage to assigned leadership is that it makes it difficult for the group to confront an inadequate leader. The person's power is seen as coming "from above" and Roman Catholics have long been trained to feel helpless in the light of such "givenness." This places the responsibility for the function and performance of a leader on the director of the program, an awesome burden in a program with eleven groups.

Even given these disadvantages, assigned leadership seemed the best way to begin. The community with which we were dealing simply had not been enabled to the point where they could assume, accept, or assign leadership without the greater authority of pastor and church. However, leadership assigned by the group itself developed naturally in those groups that met over an extended period of time.

Although we did not attempt rotating leadership in our first two years, the model has been used with success since. This model gives families a strong sense of ownership, an appreciation for the role of leader that encourages greater participation, and the chance for the group to experience different styles of leadership. On the minus side, it limits the amount of training leaders receive, requires continual emotional adjustment on the part of the group to new leaders, and often pressures people to assume a role in which they feel totally inadequate.

Characteristics of a Good Leader

The most important ingredient for a leader in any group dynamic situation is personal emotional health.[2] This is especially true in an area where leaders are called to share their power with people of all ages. The situation requires that people be open and caring, attentive to feelings, capable of dealing with conflicts, and willing to share on a personal level. All of this requires self-knowledge and security.

Since the central purpose of FIRE is growth in faith, leaders need to have a strong commitment to growth in their own faith life. It is enough to be searching; none of us has arrived. However, it is important that faith overflow in joyful expression. As Paul VI so beautifully expressed:

> May the world of our time, which is searching, sometimes with anguish, sometimes with hope, be enabled

to receive the Good News not from evangelizers who are dejected, discouraged, impatient or anxious, but from ministers of the gospel whose lives glow with fervor, who have first received the joy of Christ, and who are willing to risk their lives so that the Kingdom may be proclaimed...[3]

Leaders need to be people who understand how families function and who are comfortable in a family situation. They do not necessarily have to be parents, but they need to be able to work well with families and have a vested interest in the development of children. One single woman, in explaining on her evaluation why she joined FIRE, said: "I like to watch children grow. I like to feel I have some part in that growth. There are things I learn just from being with them." This type of single person can, and did, make an excellent FIRE leader.

Leaders need to be aware of their own values and beliefs and have a basic respect for those that differ from theirs. Even in a church with as authoritative a belief structure as Roman Catholicism, there is much room for differences in belief and practice. Leaders need to be people who can accept that two different points of view can both be right, that they do not have to impose their point of view in order to prove that it is correct.

On a very practical level, leaders need to have the time and motivation for the training and preparation that will be required of them.

Leadership Recruitment

This was a comparatively simple task in establishing the FIRE program. There was already a group of families meeting in the parish to pray and do activities with their children. These people had a strong interest in sharing what they had received from this experience. Other families who had been involved in leadership positions in the existing religious education program were drawn to the family-centered aspect of the new program. Many people were willing to take on leadership roles so that the new program could become a reality for the parish. In other parishes beginning FIRE, CFM, Marriage Encounter, Parenting for Peace and Justice groups, cursillo, and religious education programs provided most of the leaders.

As the program expanded and more leaders were needed, different methods of recruitment were used. In trying to encourage group-assigned leadership, we developed a "Loan-a-Leader Program." The leader of an already existing group would take on doing the Advent Segment for a new group. The hope was that leadership would emerge within the group during this period. It didn't happen, probably because the presence of "experienced" leaders inhibited this. What happened was that the group opted for rotating leadership. Within a period of rotation, leadership frequently emerged. Two groups remained quite successfully with the concept of rotating leadership.

However leaders are chosen, it is absolutely essential to have your initial leaders before you open the program to the parish or have your initial explanation session. If you wait to see "how many people will sign up," there is a strong temptation to simply ask everyone who joined if he or she would be willing to lead. This means that leaders are not really screened very effectively and this led to problems, both in the original parish and in churches that have adopted the program since.

An initial training session held in September for all those asked to even consider leading, can be a wonderful way to convince people to lead. It will begin to foster community and will offer the opportunity to explain FIRE in depth to a whole group in the parish. If the group leaves excited, they will spread the word around the parish before the explanation session is even announced. Such an initial session can be done with other churches in the area that are also planning on using the program, or it can be sponsored by a diocese. Which brings us into our next topic...

Leadership Training

Given all the above characteristics of the good leader, there are still basic skills that need to be developed in those recruited. The theology within each lesson needs to be explained in depth. In an inductive learning situation, a lesson has the opportunity to go in many more different directions than are possible in a typical deductive class. Although leaders are never expected to be answer people, they need to be adequately equipped to handle theological situations that arise.

Most of the original FIRE leaders had never had the opportunity to work in an intergenerational setting. While the lessons were structured for them to appeal to all ages, leaders still needed to develop the ability to draw all ages into an experience. Part of this comes naturally to parents, since they do this in every family activity but they needed to learn how to use those family skills in a group setting.

We found that the most effective way to do this was to actually do the experience with the leaders and their families, modeling for them the way to conduct an experience in an intergenerational setting. This gave them the opportunity to enjoy the lesson as participants with the freedom to concentrate on their own children. It gave all of us, myself included, the chance to see what questions would arise naturally as a result of the experience and how we would deal with them.

We met as leaders once for every two home group meetings. This did not allow us to do every experience, and so I concentrated on the ones I felt would cause difficulty. After doing the lesson together, the older children would take the younger ones to another area for refreshments and a story, record or film. The leaders would then discuss the theology involved and how things were going in their groups. Other leaders could give a struggling leader input on how to deal with a difficult situation. Triumphs and tragedies were shared.

During a leader meeting, the leaders were provided with the program materials and background reading. They were encouraged to read a lesson and begin preparation at least one week before their group met. This gave them the opportunity to internalize the concepts and see how they were happening in their own lives.

By the middle of the second year, the leaders no longer felt it was necessary to do the experience. Leader meetings became largely adult gatherings with time spent discussing alternatives and adaptations for various groups, reviewing theology, sharing successes and failures, and praying together. Leaders came to see themselves in a shepherding role, bearing the burdens of their communities in their hearts. In the process, they became a strong, cohesive community, evidenced by the fact that those who left leadership positions continued to come to the leader meetings.

This support was so essential that I would encourage churches to begin with at least two FIRE groups to provide the leaders with support. If this is impossible, I would encourage leaders to meet with those in a neighboring church.

Some churches that have used FIRE since that original group have offered three day-long training sessions each year, at the beginning of each liturgical segment. This can be very effective, since it allows a church to gather with other churches using the program and bring in someone in who is well versed in the process and has a strong background in theology. The leadership training video also provides more in-depth understanding. However, neither obviates the necessity of on-going leader meetings for prayer and support.

Communities grow and die on the strength of their leaders. For a pastor or DRE to place a set of FIRE lessons in someone's hands and expect that person to function as leader is to place far too much faith in the written program and far too little importance on the human element.

Large Group

The purpose of the large group activities in FIRE was to make people aware of belonging to a larger community: first, the FIRE group community and secondly, the Church. It gave people the opportunity to celebrate what they held in common, enabling them to see that that is one of the major tasks of the Church. This was done basically through two types of activities: social and liturgical.

Social Activities

Social activities in FIRE can be unique to individual parishes. They are determined by location, size of the group, facilities available, and the interests within a particular area. Our church did not have the space to handle any large group social activities, which ruled out things like pot luck suppers and family film nights.

Our social activities were determined mainly by the young people in the program. Mid-year was celebrated with a roller skating party. A roller skating rink in Waterbury rented out its entire facility to interested groups. This was close enough distance-wise and within our budget. It also offered space for the group to sit and share a meal together.

A state park in town provided the facility for our closing activity. Families gathered to share a pot luck picnic. This activity was developed under the new pastors to include an outdoor liturgy. Everyone was free to invite friends not in FIRE to these activities, and several new families were introduced to the program in this manner. However, the primary intent was to give those in FIRE a larger experience of community.

Liturgical Celebrations

> Catechesis has the task of preparing individuals for knowing, active, and fruitful liturgical and sacramental celebration and for profound reflection upon it.[4]

It is the teaching of the Roman Catholic Church that liturgy actually accomplishes the saving acts it symbolizes. Therefore, if we wish a community to experience itself as saved, we invite them to celebrate the paschal mystery that both proclaims that reality and mediates it.

FIRE celebrated four formal liturgical services within the context of the program:

1. The Covenant Celebration: a Liturgy of the Word held at the beginning of the year. In this celebration, the group members' commitment to each other was formalized and blessed and the leaders were commissioned.

2. Penance Service: a more formal Liturgy of the Word during which the sacrament of Reconciliation was celebrated. It was normally held just before the Lenten Segment, since this is the proper liturgical time for penance.

3. Calvary Walk: a paraliturgical service based on the stations of the cross. It was prepared for the FIRE

group by the teens in the program, and was celebrated by the entire parish on the Friday before Good Friday.

4. Closing Liturgy: a Eucharistic celebration held as close to Pentecost as possible. It marked the end of the Easter season. Children in FIRE who were receiving Eucharist for the first time were invited to celebrate at this Liturgy.

With the exception of the Calvary Walk, all of the liturgies were followed with refreshments.

In addition to the liturgies planned and sponsored by FIRE, some of the groups became involved, as a group, in preparing the liturgies for Holy Week. Several made a point of attending the same Sunday liturgy and going out for coffee together or meeting in one another's homes. Sacred Heart was a liturgically rich parish and FIRE became involved, as a community, in many of the liturgical opportunities that were offered by the church as a whole. The most impressive of these was the chance to participate in the Rite of Christian Initiation of Adults for those FIRE members who chose to become part of the Roman Catholic Church.

In a liturgically poor community, FIRE can offer people the opportunity to experience good paraliturgical services. This can eventually have an influence on the parish liturgy.

Background Sessions

At the end of the Introductory Segment of FIRE, I visited each of the groups and discussed with them what they felt they needed in the future. Many of the adults expressed the desire for an in-depth theological treatment of the subject covered in the sessions. Their experiences had created a hunger in them that was not being satisfied within the structure of the program. Such an in-depth discussion of the topic was more than the leaders were equipped to handle and more than the children were willing to endure.

It was decided to create three adult, large group sessions for Year I. (Older children desiring to attend were welcome.) These sessions were not required for participation in the program; they were simply offered for those who were interested. The first examined the idea of prophecy in Israel in greater depth and explored the growth of the concept of Messiah. The second dealt with the historical truth of the gospels and showed the development of New Testament Christology from Mark through John. The third was a session in ecclesiology and examined the idea of church as presented in the two Council documents on the subject.

The first background session was attended by six adults (one of whom became sick in the middle of the session and had to leave). We taped the session and circulated the tape among the FIRE families. The second session was attended by thirty-two very enthused people. The impact of the session on the group as a whole was best evidenced by the fact that the third session was attended by 87 of the 125 adults in FIRE. The following year, the background sessions were offered to the entire parish.

The home group sessions in FIRE whet people's appetite for God, but they obviously did not satisfy the hunger they created. As people came to experience God in their lives, they wanted to know more about God, about Scripture, about the church. The *General Catechetical Directory* sees adult education as standing at the center of the church's educational mission. Ongoing adult education and formation are absolutely necessary to any catechetical endeavor. Background sessions were FIRE's way of participating in this vision.

Time Line

The following time line demonstrates the way in the which FIRE was developed in Sacred Heart Parish and includes some of the adjustments made by other churches that chose to use the program.

Year I

June: Initial parish meeting to decide the feasibility of a family/intergenerational program. In Sacred Heart Parish, this was a parish meeting to which all members of the church were invited and the future of religious education in the parish was discussed. In other parishes that have used the program since, this initial meeting was held primarily with the Christian Education Board.

July: This period of time was used to begin to spread the idea by word of mouth and to discover possible leaders for the groups.

August: Information regarding the new program was presented in the bulletin and explained from the altar. Leaders were chosen.

September: An initial meeting was held for all interested adults. This meeting explained the theological and philosophical rationale underlying the program and the dynamics of the program. It included an experience that enabled people to taste what the meetings would be like. At the end of this meeting, people were asked to register if they were interested in participating in the two-year pilot.

October: Home groups were formed.

November: Leader meetings began. The talk was given on family spirituality for the parents in FIRE.

December: An Advent celebration was held for all the families at church. We gathered in our groups to make ornaments for the Jesse tree. Each group explained their biblical person and hung their ornament during a Liturgy. The first-year evaluation of FIRE led to dropping this element.

January: The Planning Committee (described in Components) met to plan the Introductory Segment of FIRE. The primary purpose of this segment was simply to begin the process of forming a community and give families a chance to experience what this program would entail. While it introduces them to Scripture reading and the process of "doing" theology, the theological content of these sessions was intentionally kept light.

Lent: Throughout February and March, the groups met for four home sessions. The leaders met once before every two sessions for training and once before the final session which was held after Easter.

May: A closing Eucharistic Liturgy was celebrated for all the families. Leaders met for a day of prayer and evaluation.

Year II

June: New families wishing to join the program were invited to an orientation session. Registration for all religious education programs was held. Seventy-two households signed up for FIRE, making it necessary to form new groups and train new leaders.

Summer: The Planning Committee met weekly for three hours to pray and write the experiences for the first full year. This group continued to meet weekly throughout the year, and served as my advisory committee.

August: Home groups met to write a covenant.

September: A large group covenant celebration was held at church. Leader training sessions began. Again, the leaders met once for every two sessions they would lead. For this segment, all the leader meetings were held before the home groups began to meet. At the end of the training period, the leaders decided that they preferred to meet throughout the segment, before each pair of home group meetings. That method was employed throughout the years I conducted the program.

October—
December: Home groups met to do the first six experiences

November: Background session for adults (explained in Components).

January: Families with children preparing to receive the sacrament of Reconciliation for the first time met together three times. A Reconciliation Service was celebrated by all the families in FIRE.

Lent: Home groups met to do the five lessons of the Lenten Segment.

February: Background session for adults.

March: Confirmation students met twice to prepare the Calvary Walk (see Lesson VI of the Lenten Segment). On the Friday before Good Friday, all the FIRE families and many other families from the parish prayed the Calvary Walk together.

Eastertime: Home groups met four times to do the lessons of the Easter Segment; leaders met twice to prepare and pray.

April: Large group skating party. Background session for adults.

May: Families of children preparing to receive Eucharist for the first time met twice.

June: Closing Eucharist celebration followed by a party.

Sample Lesson: Resurrection

Introductory Segment, Experience V

The five lessons of the Introductory Segment were kept intentionally light in theological content. Their main purpose was to give people a taste of intergenerational learning and begin the process of forming community.

Theological Background

If Christ has not been raised, then our preaching is in vain and your faith is in vain. (I Cor 15:14)

The resurrection is at the heart of Christian belief. In the resurrection, death, which had been the sign of sin in the world (Romans 5:12) became the expression of divine love and the revelation of divine grace.[5] Within the ongoing reality of resurrection, Christ continues to reveal himself and to redeem the world. In the Roman Catholic liturgy, the Anamnesis states: "Christ has died, Christ is risen, Christ will come again." What is of utmost importance is that the revelational process of resurrection, first accomplished in Christ is now participated in by all Christians.[6] As Ronald Lawler so beautifully expresses:

> It is the risen Jesus himself who gives persons of faith the ability to experience his presence. He does this by allowing them to share in his own life, bringing them even now, in their lives here on earth, into a real participation in his new way of existence. This he does by bringing the faithful to a true mystical death, burial,

resurrection, and ascension with him in order that they might receive, as members of his mystical body, a share in his Spirit. ...The resurrection of Jesus is the foundation of the Christian life of faith, prayer, and spiritual growth.[7]

It is our participation in resurrection and what that means for our lives here on earth that will be the main point of this lesson. I am not unaware of the problems with the resurrection narratives, exegesis on the topic, and the works of such scholars as Raymond Brown, Pierre Benoit, and Reginald Fuller. I simply choose not to engage in the discussion at this time. Remaining true to the inductive mode of learning in FIRE involves considering first how we experience resurrection and what it means to us. Future years in the program will address the historical reality of Jesus' resurrection, how it was experienced by the early church, and how it came to be narrated in the New Testament.

Remote Preparation:

This lesson was done in a community of seven families. To facilitate the process, they were divided into four intergenerational groups. An area was prepared for each group with crayons, the color code for using them and the circle graph (given in the appendix with this lesson), a piece of scrap paper for each person, a flat area or table space to work on, and adequate lighting. In the main gathering place, a small table was prepared with a candle, the Resurrection Parable (also included) and a Bible.

I prepared myself by reading and praying over the resurrection narratives in all four gospels. I spent the week before the meeting looking for signs of resurrection in my own life. This became a supper table topic of discussion, so that my own family was prepared to share at the meeting.

Introduction:

1. Our group always began each of its meetings by assembling a wooden rainbow. Our name is "The Rainbow Connection." Each family has an arc, and as they added it to the bow, we all joined in prayer for that particular family. This period of prayer is essential to "letting go" of all the distractions we bring with us.

2. We spoke briefly about the Easter liturgy which we had all recently experienced.

3. We took a moment to review the refrain to "I am the Bread of Life" by Suzanne Toolan so that we would sing it easily later in the evening.

4. Finally, we divided the group into four subgroups by "counting down."

Experience:

1. Everyone in the group was asked to get themselves into an imaginary scenario. The wage earner in the family had been offered a new job. It was the best possible opportunity. The benefits were great, the educational opportunities were wonderful, the pay was wonderful. The area offered excellent opportunities for the rest of the family. There was one problem, though. It was in a foreign country. No one they knew had ever been there. If they chose to go, they would probably never come back.

2. The group was asked to consider this possibility in their four small groups. Each group was to be an imaginary family. The first step in deciding what to do was to get in touch with their own feelings. Here it was emphasized that feelings are neither right nor wrong. They just are. To help them express what they were feeling, they were asked to draw a per-

son, using the color code given at each of their group work spaces. Each color represented a feeling. Their head might be orange (excitement) but their heart might be purple (loneliness). They were then sent to work in their groups, with a fifteen minute time limit for drawing. Everyone was reminded that art did not count.

3. While the groups were working, I went around and gave further instructions to one adult. As they finished their people, all were to share their drawing and their feelings about the proposed move. A decision concerning the move was to be reached by consensus and the circle was to be filled in with colors representing everyone's feelings.

4. The adults were a little hesitant at first about coloring. The children moved right into it and showed real delight at the opportunity to express their feelings so graphically. Children three and up wanted the colors read to them, or needed to be guided with questions about how they felt, with appropriate colors pointed out. Very young ones were content to color. Some of the children needed to be assured over and over again that they would have some say in the decision. It was not until this point that I recognized that along with teaching resurrection and fostering the acceptance of feelings, we were also modeling family decision making. As the groups began sharing their figures and their feelings, I was struck by the amazement on some of the children's faces. Some of the younger ones had obviously never heard adults express fear, sadness, loneliness. It was difficult to move them on to the next part of the exercise.

5. Once the decisions were made and the circles colored, the groups returned to share with the larger group. They simply held up their graph and stated their decision. Their feelings were obvious from the colors in their circle. Three of the groups were going, but with great reluctance. One group

had been unable to reach consensus and so responded that they were undecided.

6. At this point I changed the story. I told them that their very best friend, someone who had loved them from birth and only wanted what was best for them, was president of the new company and was inviting them to come. Did it change how they felt? Did it change the decision? There was a deep silence in the group. It was broken when one of the teenagers said: "I'd feel called." The adults, who had been so hesitant to use crayons, wanted to go back and get them so that they could add more blue (peacefulness) to their circles. The group that was undecided stayed that way, but said they felt more comfortable with the possibility.

7. Every change in life is a type of death experience. It involves letting go of one thing so that we can experience new life. Jesus has gone before us in this. That is the meaning of resurrection. He is the friend who has gone first to prepare the way for us. It doesn't always change the way we feel, but it helps, just as it did tonight.

8. At this point, the group was invited to think of the deaths and resurrections they had experienced in life. My own family shared some of their experiences and this started discussion. An eight-year-old shared how she had recently moved, and this had been a death experience. A five-year-old talked about getting on a bike after a bad fall. The adults shared some of the more traumatic events in life that had led to new life. The discussion took a few moments to get started, but once started, the group could have gone on for an hour.

9. The next part of the evening was a trip backward through all their deaths and resurrections. We lowered the lights and began slowly to point out that moving is a death experience. Leaving a job or leaving college is a death experience. Starting high school, starting elementary school, are death experiences. We leave behind the security of the life

we know in the hope that the new life will be better. Giving up a crib for a big bed, a bottle for a cup, are death experiences. They are a "letting go" in the hope of greater freedom. Being born is a death experience.

10. At this point, we turned off all the lights and left only the lighted candle. I invited everyone to go back to his mother's womb. What did they feel or experience there? In the darkness, people shared single words: "Warm," "Wet," "Secure," "Loved." They talked about hearing a heartbeat. Someone questioned how you would know it was a heartbeat. One person insisted that she would know it was her mother's heart. This was the perfect lead in to the Resurrection Parable, which three of us read quietly, one as narrator, and two taking the parts of the twins.

A Resurrection Parable

Once upon a time, twins were conceived in the same womb. As time passed, they grew and began to have feelings and some idea of their surroundings.

One said, "Lucky are we to have been conceived and to have this world." The other said, "Blessed is the Mother who gave us this life and each other."

Arms grew, and fingers, legs, and toes. They explored their world and in it they found the cord which gave them life from the precious Mother's blood. So they sang: "How great is the Mother that she shares all that she has with us." And they were pleased and satisfied with their lot.

Months passed and they noticed changes.

"We are changing. What can it mean?"

"It means that birth is coming near."

Fear crept over them. Birth meant that they had to leave all their world behind them.

"If it were up to me, I'd live here forever," said one.

"We must be born," said the other. "See the scars? There were others here before us. Maybe there's life after birth."

"How can there be life after birth? Have you ever talked to anyone who's been born? Has anyone ever re-entered the womb after birth? This life is absurd if it all ends in birth. If this is so, then there really is no Mother." "But of course there is a Mother. Who else gives us nourishment and this world?"

"We get our own nourishment and our world has always been here. If there is a Mother, where is she? Have you ever seen her or talked to her? We just invented her because it makes us feel good!"

And so one complained and despaired, but the other placed its trust in the hands of the Mother. Pretty soon they knew that birth was at hand. They were scared. They cried as they were born into the light. Then they opened their eyes and found themselves cradled in the warm love of the Mother. All too wonderful to believe.[8]

As the parable ended, I added softly: "And Jesus said 'All those who believe in me, even if they die, they will live forever.'"

At this point, I began singing the refrain practiced earlier:

"And I will raise them up

And I will raise them up

And I will raise them up on the last day."

(Copyright: Suzanne M. Toolan, 1971 *Songs of Praise I*, Servant Publications)

The group joined in the singing softly. As it finished, the room was in deep and prayerful silence. We waited a full five minutes and then turned the lights up gradually. Many of the adults were in tears: even the children were peaceful.

11. The Take Home was given and the group broke up, still very subdued, to look for resurrection in their lives that week.

I have done this experience in several groups since the first one. It never fails to move people to deep silence. Hopefully, in the silence, they have the opportunity to encounter the risen Christ, so that their faith need not be dependent on the empty tomb.

Take Home

Our Easter lesson was adult-centered because resurrection is an adult concept. We are hoping that you will take time at home to celebrate resurrection on a simpler level. Here are some suggestions.

1. Take a walk outside and look for all the signs of new life coming up around you. If you have children, talk with them about the death of nature that occurs each fall and the rebirth that happens in spring. Bring some things back to form a centerpiece for your table.

2. Simply start a centerpiece and invite family members and friends to add to it on their own. (Better warn little ones not to bring cocoons into the house or you may have more life than you bargained for.)

3. Plant seeds. Take a few moments to explain to children how the new life we have been given is like the seed.

4. Look for deaths and resurrections in your own life this week. Discuss them with your family at supper or record them in your journal. Point out to others the new life you see in them.

5. Easter is an excellent time to talk with little ones about where their life came from.

6. Read the Pentecost story (Acts 2) with your family before the closing liturgy.

Notes

1. Rodney W. Napier and Matt; K. Gershenfeld *Groups: Theory and Experience*. (Boston; Houghton Mifflin Company, 1973) p. 138.

2. Margaret Sawin. *Family Enrichment with Family Clusters*. (Valley Forge: Judson Press, 1979) p. 101.

3. Paul VI. *On Evangelization in the Modern World* (8 December 1975) #80.

4. National Catechetical Directory *op.cit.* #44.

5. Karl Rahner. *On the Thelogy of Death*. (New York: Herder and Herder, 1961) p. 78.

6. Gabriel Moran. *Theology of Revelation*. (New York Seabury, 1966) p. 75.

7. Ronald Lawler, O.F.M.Cap. Thomas Comerford Lawl Wuerl, Donald W. *The Teaching of Christ*. (Huntington, IN: Our Sunday Visitor, 19) p. 158.

8. This story first appeared in the 1975 Easter issue *Agape* magazine. The magazine has since gone out of business and I have been unable to find the copyright owner or the author.

4

Evaluation

G.K. Chesterton once said, "Anything worth doing is worth doing poorly." We frequently learn more from our mistakes than from our successes. It is the things that don't work that encourage us to find new and better ways of accomplishing the same tasks. Therefore, I would strongly encourage any parish doing FIRE to evaluate frequently and change accordingly.

Evaluations can take many different forms: questionnaires, personal interviews, observation, group discussions. You will need to decide which method, or which combination of methods, will work best for you. Keep in mind the cardinal rule of evaluating: Don't Get Discouraged. Any program is only as perfect as the participants, the parish, and, of course, the director!

In evaluating the original FIRE program, several different methods were used throughout the initial process. A two page questionnaire was given to all participating households at the end of the first year. A day of planning and evaluation was held for the leaders during which they discussed the strengths and weaknesses of the program as a whole, of their individual groups, and of themselves as leaders. I personally visited and observed each of the eleven groups, discussing the impact the program was having and the needs they felt it could meet in the future. The program underwent continual adaptation based on this ongoing process.

FIRE was evaluated in much greater depth in 1987 as part of a doctoral project. I have included that information here to offer insight into some of the strengths and weaknesses of the program as well as offering ideas for your own evaluation process.

For the purposes of the doctorate, I felt that the best assessment would be obtained by questioning several of the churches presently using FIRE. Two separate questionnaires were formulated. One was addressed to members of households who have participated in FIRE; the second was addressed to administrators who have chosen to do FIRE within their churches or to include it within their college Family Ministry curriculum. In reporting the results, I have explained what I hoped to learn by each question and what I actually learned. I have compared that information, wherever possible, with the findings from the evaluation of the initial pilot.

Evaluation Response

The evaluations that I have included here were sent to four churches in three different states and to the Family Ministry Program at Fordham University. Administrators were asked to distribute group member questionnaires to two or three participants or families presently in FIRE. In addition, I distributed eight questionnaires randomly among families who had originally participated in the FIRE program at Sacred Heart Parish. All the administrators returned the evaluations and sixteen group members responded. While I recognize the limits of such a small sampling, much of the information corresponded closely with what had already been discovered by the first-year evaluation (completed by sixty-seven families) and what I had learned through interviews and observation.

Group Members

How Did You Hear About FIRE?

I am frequently asked about the best way to make FIRE known within a community. Churches beginning the program have tried mass media, sermons, meetings, etc. By asking those who chose to participate in a group how they heard about FIRE, I hoped to discover what types of publicity actually moved people to join. One hundred percent of the people who responded, both to this evaluation and the original one, had heard about the program from a friend, minister, or someone whose opinion they respected and valued. Word of mouth remains the single, most effective means for publicizing this program. I have, in the past, sold copyright permission for use of the program to churches in seven different states and three different countries, all of whom heard about it by word of mouth.

Based on this finding, I would strongly encourage any church beginning the program to spend a great deal of time talking about it. Offering leaders in the community a chance to experience FIRE through an initial workshop or visit to a session in another church will give these people the opportunity to talk about it. People in the community can be approached personally and invited to an initial meeting. New families joining the church can be introduced to the idea. The data seems to indicate that the greater the initial discussion of the program, the greater will be the participation.

Why Did You Become Involved In This Program?

In asking this question, I was concerned about how clearly I had presented the goals of the program both to group members and their pastors, and how closely the needs of the group members corresponded with the administrator's reasons for initiating FIRE. Any major discrepancy would indicate poor communication on my part or on the part of the priest/minister/director involved.

Most of those joining FIRE originally did so for the sake of their children: "because we wanted the religious education of our children to be a family experience"; "because we feel responsible for what our children learn about Jesus." Even single people chose to be involved because of the desire to work with, or just be with children: "I am interested in teaching children and these teaching methods"; "I like to be involved with young families and their religious practices." A few also wanted support communities for their children where faith could be discussed; "I became involved because I wanted my children to learn about God in a loving atmosphere with people who really believe and live their faith daily. It was important to me to have my children hear other people share their experiences of God in their life. That He made a difference."

Since FIRE is primarily an alternative form of religious education, I feel that coming "for the children" is a valid reason for joining FIRE. My own goals for the program are much deeper and my hope is that people will grow beyond that and eventually come to see all that the program offers to them as individuals and as families. Their responses to later questions indicate that this, indeed, did happen, but it was religious education for their children that first brought them to FIRE.

In choosing to do FIRE, administrators had broader goals than the families who chose to participate. While they, too, focused on the children and the idea of strengthening families, they were convinced of the benefits of an intergenerational learning experience in enabling adults to grow in their faith. They hoped to "deepen the spiritual growth" of the church with "faith overflowing into worship."

Only two administrators expressed the desire to offer an alternative to the "traditional, child-centered classroom model" of religious education. With the exception of Gloria Durka of Fordham, they seemed unable or unwilling to accept the well-documented inadequacies of the present models. The administrators also had many more hidden agendas for the program: "bring people into the church," "reach those not involved in religious ed."

One group member captured much of the essence of FIRE in her response: "It just felt right. It helped me to make the connection between the Jesus story of how to live lovingly and the ways I was a good person—and sometimes not as loving as I wanted to be—especially in ways I hadn't recognized before."

Do You Feel That Your Group Is Becoming (Has Become) A Community To Whom You Could Turn For Support? What Has Helped Or Hindered This Process?

Since the primary purpose of FIRE is to provide an inter-generational community in which faith can be experienced, this was a crucial question. In the initial evaluation done with the leaders after the Introductory Segment and in the evaluation done with the families at the end of Year I of the program, the response to this was disappointing. Most of the families, at that point, did not see themselves as a true support community. The pastor and I both saw a sense of community developing long before the group members themselves became aware of it.

Therefore, I was not surprised that those groups presently doing FIRE for the first time responded in the same way. The most typical response to the question was a guarded "somewhat." Administrators, on the other hand, gave an unequivocal "yes."

Those who had been in the original FIRE group and had remained in the program for a much longer time felt much more certain about their communities. "We will reach out to each other for prayers, advice, to discuss a problem, or if we need a good listener." "We get a lot of spiritual support, perhaps the kind that is hard to ask from family members or friends." "We feel a bond...I think that prayer brings this about." I have known FIRE groups to support a member who was out of work, help in running a fundraiser to provide a van for a handicapped child, provide meals and child care for someone who was sick. This kind of community takes a few years to develop, though. In writing about the original program, the pastor of that period says: "These groups eventually became real basic Christian communities of prayer, support, and action."

The level of commitment of individuals within the group was a factor frequently cited as helping or hindering community. My own experience with groups has shown that nothing destroys a group faster than the consistent absence of one or two families. It undermines the importance of what is happening for the rest of the group.

Social activities were also seen as important in developing community. Even though I have referred to them as "large group activities" where several FIRE groups come together, the evaluations made it clear that those social events were needed whether or not there was more than one FIRE group within a community.

Group members felt is was easier to become community if they associated with the people within their group at other times. I have found that those families who ask to be together usually experience bonding much earlier, probably because they are together in other areas of their lives.

One of the groups included in the evaluation had been formed by two churches working together. All the group members felt that this hindered the sense of community growing within the group, but that it helped the churches to grow closer. I think that I would probably share their answers with churches considering such a venture, since there seems to be both loss and gain.

In two groups, all members expressed the desire for longer meetings and more group-building activities. In both these group, leadership is alternated. I suspect that what members were seeking is a time, at the beginning of each meeting, to adjust, to the different styles of leadership. These groups also showed less community development than those with assigned leadership that had been meeting for an equal length of time. They complained of a lack of focus, something the other groups did not experience. Based on these findings, I would suggest that alternating leadership within a new group hinders the development of community. While I have enumerated the advantages of this form of leadership at an earlier point in this manual, evaluation leads me to believe that it is not as successful as assigned leadership, at least in the formational stage of the community.

Those groups that perceived themselves as communities all saw praying together as a major source of bonding, as well as sharing feelings and just talking time to get to know each other. One administrator saw the design of the program as efficacious: "The group dynamics based on sound Christian principles and good psychology 'serendipitously' built community. The process encouraged each person within the group to actively participate."

In speaking to children who had participated in the program the single factor they saw as most responsible in creating a sense of community was respect. They discussed the importance of feeling free to say what they felt and having it "count." One teenager expressed "being listened to, like a person, not just a kid." While the children developed a sense of community more rapidly than the adults, for them, too, it took longer than the Introductory Segment and Year I.

The next three questions dealt with the content and process of FIRE. The idea of the program was to make it possible for families to talk about God, relate their own personal stories to the Scripture, and hand on their values. These questions examine whether or not the program accomplishes this.

Did You Read Scripture Before Becoming Involved In This Program? Have Those Reading Habits Changed?

Not surprisingly, those who described themselves as immersed in Scripture before joining FIRE changed the least as a result of the program. They spoke of having a greater focus in their reading, of understanding better the context, particularly of the Old Testament. Group insights greatly enhanced the impact of familiar passages for some. One person who had read Scripture had been unable to share it with her family until FIRE.

Those who described themselves as reading Scripture a little or not at all before FIRE offered a mixture of responses. One described himself as having no real interest; two simply said their reading habits had not changed much. On the other hand, several responded that their habits had changed radically. "I have become much more interested in the theology, the history, Jesus as a person, Christology." "We now learn together as a family and share our feelings about Scripture." "Scripture is precious to me now."

Based on these answers, the most that I can say is that FIRE acquaints people with Scripture and offers focus and direction for those who desire to know more. It does not create that desire; it simply fosters it.

This was a slightly more negative response than that obtained in earlier evaluations. I suspect this indicates less dedication in following through with the assignments at home, since most of the scripture reading is done at home. This lack of dedication could reflect the fact that for some people responding, FIRE is simply a supplement and may not be regarded as seriously as religious education.

Do You Talk About God More As A Family Since Joining FIRE?

The answer to this question was a universal affirmative, as it has been on every evaluation I have done with FIRE groups. FIRE's greatest success appears to be in enabling "God- talk" within families. "We are more open, much more understanding, we have learned to listen to each other." "It's much more comfortable." "The lessons make it easy to focus on something specific and give beautiful ideas for daily living."

Would You Say That FIRE Has

A. Assisted You In Handing On Your Values To Your Children?

B. Challenged Your Values?

C. Both?

D. Neither?

Three families responded to this question with (a). Only one of the three offered any additional information as to how this had happened. "We can't hand on values unless we talk and since FIRE offered opportunities to refer to lessons, in this respect, it helps greatly."

All the other families responding felt that FIRE both challenged and enabled them to hand on values. "We were given new values through FIRE. Many times, it was our children who enabled us to change." "While the families had a lot of the basic values we uphold, we also learned from them, and we found ourselves re-thinking some issues and re-evaluating." "It especially helped in verbalizing our values and connecting them to Scripture."

Much of the handing on of values seems to be connected to the previous question of "God-talk." Families who can talk comfortably about God are also comfortable talking about values. This question would have been more effective, though, if I had asked all the families to share how the program had helped with value transmission, since there could be another point I am missing.

Has This Program Challenged You To Become Involved In Ministry? In Social Justice Issues? Be Specific.

Service is one of the three basic components of all valid religious education. It is not enough to hand on values if we do not live by them ourselves. This question hoped to discover whether or not the program moved people to such action.

The answers fell into two distinct groups. While everyone felt challenged and encouraged by the program to become involved in ministry, a few were still at the stage of talking about it as a family and considering where they were called to work. "As parents, we have become aware through FIRE that it isn't enough to tell children what is right, we must teach by example."

Some members had become actively involved in specific projects such as the food bank. Those who had been in the program for an extended length of time were more inclined to view all of their lives as ministry. A mother of six small children responded: "My ministry is not necessarily something that shows to the world, but a conviction in my heart that I am doing right now exactly what God wants of me. This feeling can only come after establishing a relationship with the Lord. FIRE helped me to develop a prayer life and a desire to know the Lord more deeply." A woman who works for a large company sees her ministry as the small affirmation groups she has developed at work to improve productivity. She feels that FIRE taught her the importance of feeling good about herself and it gave her the leadership skills to share that with others.

I have watched some people in the communities grow to the point where they could make a stand on social issues such as low-cost housing in the town. Again, though, this response has been very individual, and I do not wish to make any judgement on this. Grace is given differently, and we are not all called to the same type of action.

Is FIRE An Alternative Or Supplement To The Religious Education Program In Your Parish? How Do You Feel About This?

FIRE was a supplement in two of the parishes in the survey. Several members expressed no strong feelings; some expressed mild approval of this. One member suggested that it might be far more effective as an alternative. In the other two parishes, FIRE was an alternative, and people felt very strongly that this is the way it should be.

My own personal bias is that FIRE functions best where it is an alternative to the existing Christian education program. The responses to the second question regarding reasons for joining FIRE lead one to believe that most of the people involved would not have come to a program simply billed as family enrichment. Making FIRE an alternative affirms their ability to teach their children themselves and underlines that what they are doing is really important. Parents feel it is important to consider the demands made by the program. "It has to be an alternative because there has to be total commitment, from parents and children alike, for it to succeed." "Two programs would have been too much for the children." Our own experience the first year of allowing families to choose it as supplement or alternative made it abundantly clear that families were far more committed when the program was chosen as an alternative.

This presents a serious problem within the Protestant churches where "Sunday School" serves the dual purpose of religious education and babysitting for the worship service. Creative approaches to the problem will need to be considered. It may even require seriously examining the goals of worship within a community and determining why these necessitate excluding children.

What Do You See As The Specific Strengths Of This Program?

Everyone involved in FIRE, administrators and members alike, saw the impact on the family as one of its greatest strengths.

"It helps families to pray together, to share with other people, to be more open, to grow." (member)

"The fact that the family attends together creates a unity, a oneness, one accord." (member)

"The children become more comfortable expressing their feelings about God and they see their parents doing so." (member)

"Good forum to emphasize family beliefs." (member)

"Puts Christian Education back in the family where it belongs." (administrator)

"This program has provided family ministers and directors of religious education programs with hope for the feasibility of implementing programs which are truly systems-oriented and which are geared to enriching the family as a system." (Gloria Durka. Family Minister Director, Fordham University)

"It rests upon and presents the conviction that religious education is a family affair while providing tools needed to enable the family to implement a family-centered approach." (administrator)

The theological content and experiential method were the second most frequently mentioned strengths.

"...its approach—affecting children and adults alike—meeting them where they are at." (member)

"sound theology" (member)

"learning experience in a fun situation" (member)

"Its experiential approach is its greatest strength—leading people to think and own in their hearts the story." (member)

"good theological method" (administrator)

"sound educational and theological principles...truly a participatory model" (Durka)

Among those who had been meeting over a longer period of time, the sense of community, spirit of prayer, and freedom were mentioned as strengths.

What Are Its Greatest Weaknesses?

The most commonly mentioned weakness was the need for commitment for the program to succeed. Several people, after writing that, were able to see this as a weakness within the community, leadership, etc. rather than the program. I do not apologize for the fact that FIRE calls people to commitment and requires that of them. Christianity is a demanding faith. Two administrators saw the lack of committed, prayerful people to lead within the community as a problem, but not as a specific weakness of the program. The unwillingness of parents to take on the responsibility for educating their children was also mentioned in this context. While FIRE seeks to encourage people and affirm their ability to educate their children, it does not make light of this responsibility.

A more legitimate weakness mentioned was the strong "family" orientation of the language. While I define "family" at the outset as any household (single people, married people, one and two parent families), the word simply cannot be stretched in that manner. It does not change the experience of "family" of those receiving the program. This deserves careful attention, and many of the Take Home experiences were re-written to be more inclusive.

Weaknesses mentioned by individuals were: "not enough memorization and content," "some truths do not lend themselves to experiential method," "structure not always evident to parents who may feel their children are not getting 'it,'" "some people are not ready for it."

Choose One FIRE Lesson That You (Your Family) Especially Enjoyed. Why Was The Experience Enjoyable? What Do You Feel You Learned From It?

In asking the families to do this, I was attempting to determine if any particular type of lesson was more significant or more helpful. Every lesson was chosen by at least one person. Respondents tended to choose a group of lessons. Those more into the prayerful aspects of the program chose Creation, Jeremiah, Ezekiel, all designed to be basically prayer experiences. Those who were more content-oriented chose the radio plays, John the Baptist, Pentecost. Those whose basic orientation was social justice chose Prophecy, Jesus As Human, and The Kingdom. Rather than pointing out for me the particular type of lesson that succeeded best, this question convinced me that many types of lessons are needed to accommodate the different needs of the people involved. In a group where people are at many different ages and stages of development, it could hardly be otherwise.

Administrator Response

I have already addressed the administrators' responses to all those questions included on both questionnaires. Two questions involving leadership and one involving the impact on the church as a whole were addressed exclusively to the administrators.

Do You Feel Your Leaders Were Adequately Trained?

With the exception of the parish where FIRE was done originally, all the leaders in the Churches included in the evaluation were trained in one-day workshops. While the administrators all expressed the belief that this was adequate training, they also felt that lack of spiritual commitment and good theological background were weaknesses in their leaders.

In the original parish, leaders were trained in ongoing leader meetings with prayer and theological input. Of these, the pastor says: "The leaders were well trained. I strongly believe this was due in great part to the comprehensive monthly training sessions which always had good theological input and provided spiritual support."

Our experience was that the leaders needed the support of other leaders. The leader's group became their community, rather than the communities they led. Within the leader community, they were challenged to grow spiritually as well as theologically. I suspect that the lack of such on-going support is partly responsible for the weaknesses the other administrators cite in their leaders.

This type of support can be more difficult to provide in a church that has only one FIRE group. This is where I feel a church could benefit most by joining with one or two neighboring churches. The FIRE communities could be composed of individuals from one church, but the leader's group would be made up of the leaders from all the churches.

This, of course, assumes a designated leadership, since no community could evolve without continuity. Considering the results of these evaluations, I would strongly recommend such leadership for the first two years of the program.

Has This Program Impacted Your Church As A Whole In Any Way?

Good religious education overflows to the community. Like the process of becoming a community, though, it is a slow process. Those who were finishing Year I of FIRE saw a slight impact on the church: people asking about the program, a sense of ownership in the church, but, as one minister put it, "It is certainly not happening like lightening." I suspect it is too soon and the programs are still too small to tell.

In Sacred Heart, where the program originated and lasted for many years, the former pastor writes:

> One of the greatest impacts was demonstrated at our 10:00 a.m. Liturgy. Most of the people in this program participated in the Eucharist. They did this knowing that the others would be there. As a result, they brought much to this Liturgy, and the spirit was felt by most parishioners at this Mass. Also, the program instilled a conviction of commitment and missionary spirit. Thus, those who were in the program became the real "workers" in the parish. Parishioners also were quick to notice how these groups cared for each other and tried to "make real" their Christianity. All this was done in such a fashion to cause no divisions or cliques.

Having studied the responses of all those presently doing FIRE, I would make the following recommendations to those who choose to do it in the future. I would recommend strongly that churches offer FIRE as an alternative religious education program, that they assign leadership for the first two years, and that they offer their leaders some form of ongoing support and theological training. I also think it is worth pointing out to churches beginning the program that the formation of community takes time, at least two years, according to our survey, and not to look for instant results.

One of the principal goals of FIRE that was not included in the evaluation process was the interiorization of faith. I felt that this was largely immeasurable, but did some research on those who had already attempted to study this in other areas. I came across work done by a graduate student at Fairfield University who had designed an evaluation for the Renew program (a Scripture sharing process) that attempted to determine whether or not Renew enabled people to internalize their faith. The study showed that Renew had been ineffective in this regard, but I was not sure if this reflected the effectiveness of the program or the effectiveness of the tool. One thing I realized in studying this research paper was that if I wanted to attempt to analyze the interiorization of faith by FIRE members, it would be an enormous task, far beyond the scope of this evaluation.

However, one very interesting piece of information emerged from the work of this student. Several groups from the Bridgeport and Hartford diocese had been included in the study, one of them a FIRE group doing Renew with its adults. In a cover letter to the Hartford director of Renew, the researcher points out:

> There were two groups that had a higher than average rating on the internalized responses. One was from Hartford (archdiocese) and one was from Bridgeport (diocese). A little detective work turned up a correlation. Both of these groups were part of small faith sharing communities. The highest was the Hartford group. This group has participated in the FIRE program (a program written and copyrighted by Kathleen Chesto of Sacred Heart Parish, Southbury). They were the group that demonstrated the highest degree of "connection to Jesus" in their responses.
> —Ellie Hawthorne

Within my own family, I have seen a high degree of this internalization in my children. I include them as part of this evaluation because they have participated in FIRE since its beginning. I recognize that part of their response is due to what we have done as parents and not just to their participation in the program, but this would be true for any family. It is, in fact, the whole basis of FIRE, that what happens in the family is far more important than anything we can teach. This is why we chose to focus on families.

The year that we did "The Convention at Jordan," we were left without a home for four months. It was necessary for the five of us to live in two small rooms in a friend's basement. All three children quickly identified for us, their frantic parents, that this was our sojourn in the desert. They were able to identify our Whiner (Why did we ever leave Oxford?), our strategist or Jahwist (I think I can get enough rooms on the new house finished by April...), our Nomads (I like living in this basement here in the middle of town) and our priest (If we just keep trusting the Lord...). Each time someone mentioned what it had been like in our old home, all three children would chime in, "Oh for the leeks and garlics of Egypt." It brought sanity to an insane period of life.

As my fifteen-year-old son prepared for Confirmation last November, we had a long discussion about his choice of the Catholic Church. I wrote down a portion of that discussion and saved it and include it here as evidence of his deeply thoughtful approach.

> You know, Mom, all religion is basically self-seeking. The fact that I choose to be Catholic does not have much to do with how I feel about God. I could love God and be anything or nothing at all. We belong to a religion because it satisfies our need to be part of a group that thinks like we do, or maybe it makes us feel good, or assures us of going to heaven. It helps us to make sense out of life. Some religions are more self-seeking than others though. Like our friends (here he mentioned a family who belong to a Pentecostal Holiness group). Their religion just wants to make them holy. It doesn't even want them to associate with the rest of us. Roman Catholicism sees itself as responsible for the whole world, not just faith-wise either. The Catholic church sees itself as needing to do something about hunger and justice and all those things. It doesn't always act that way on a local level (look at our church!), but at least it proclaims it! I choose to be

Catholic because it is the least self-seeking religion I know."

As a mother, I have to admit I would have liked to have heard something about Jesus and a little more about prayer, but he has certainly made his faith his own and knows what he considers important.

Recently, our fourteen-year-old daughter was asked to write an essay for English on the most memorable day of her life, describing it as either a day of thorns and iron or a day of gold and flowers. She chose the day her father told her that I had multiple sclerosis. She shared her terrible struggle to make sense of it all and her own growth in the process. In the end, her lived faith shines through.

> I don't know why God allows these things to happen, but maybe it is because of the good that comes out of them. We have grown so much closer as a family, and I know now that I have the strength to handle any- thing that might happen to me in life. I can't say that my day of iron and thorns turned into gold and flowers, but it's a mixture. Maybe that's the way life is supposed to be, iron and thorns, gold and flowers.

FIRE has already accomplished much of the internaliza- tion task in my own family. I have also had the privilege of watching this happen in the lives of other families in my community. I know that it is possible to create more vibrant, faith-filled learning situations, and I encourage others to try.

5

Convincing The Parish

Once you have become convinced of the value of an intergenerational or family program, it is still necessary to convince the parish. Your role in doing this will depend largely on your role in the parish. But whether you are a pastor trying to convince parents and religious education personnel, a DRE trying to convince pastor and parents, or parents struggling for a more vibrant religious education program for your families, many of the questions you face will be the same.

Will The Children Learn The Basic Truths About The Faith?

FIRE does not involve the amount of memory work or the question and answer approach of many of the other religious education programs on the market, making this a common concern. FIRE is based on the National Catechetical Directory and covers the main truths of the faith in a four-year cycle. How well these truths are learned depends, as it does in any religious education program, on the commitment level of the family, FIRE has the advantage of involving the whole family thus increasing the chance of follow-through at home.

Morality in FIRE is not taught as a separate section, but as the result of beliefs and convictions expressed throughout the four years. Moral issues are examined in lessons on Jesus, Moses, prophecy in Israel, etc. as well as in lessons exploring family rules, the Sermon on the Mount, and the Commandments.

How Much Does FIRE Cost?

The cost of the FIRE program for an entire parish is less than the cost would be for typical text books for the children in any one FIRE group. Materials for the projects described can usually be salvaged from common household items and suggestions are given to help you do this.

Should FIRE Supplement The Existing Religious Education Program, Replace It, Or Be Offered As An Alternative?

FIRE works best when it is offered as an alternative to the existing religious education program in the parish, rather than as a *replacement*. Because it demands a greater involvement and time commitment on the part of parents, they will resent having it forced on them as the only available form of religious education. Many people feel they are not at a point in their lives where they can participate in this type of program, and it is important for us to respect this.

All of us, generally, are much more supportive of a program when we are allowed to choose to participate. Offering FIRE as an alternative is also giving people the freedom to choose the existing program, which could, in turn, generate more support for that program also.

The one exception to this general rule is the very small parish that cannot possibly maintain two programs. In such a case, the people of the parish need to be involved much more directly in choosing the program and in deciding if they truly want FIRE as their total religious education process.

FIRE does not usually work well as a *supplement* because it involves too great a time commitment. Absenteeism becomes a problem since a "supplement" tends to be viewed as something that isn't totally necessary. This can be very destructive to the developing sense of community in a small group. In a supplemental program, there is also a tendency to neglect the Take Home assignments, resulting in the loss of one of the greatest benefits of FIRE, the increase in God-talk in the home.

If parishes want to do FIRE as a supplement, I recommend that they do it as two or three family retreats per year. The experiences of each liturgical segment can be built into a retreat day, with some simplification, or into an entire weekend, with some expansion to include liturgy, quiet time, and recreation.

What Is The Best Way To Introduce FIRE To A Parish?

The most important step in introducing FIRE to a parish is to find out the needs of the people. This does not have to involve a lengthy needs assessment process. An evaluation of the existing religious education program or parish programs for the year will reveal whether or not the goals of FIRE are already being met. Are families satisfied with their ability to talk about God and share faith within the family setting? Are people looking for a way to relate what they know about God to their everyday living? Are families looking for a way to strengthen communication, decision-making and affirmation within their homes? Are people searching for a faith experience in a communal context? Is God important in their lives? Do they want to learn more about God, Scripture, and tradition? Is religion fun?

If your parish is already meeting 100% of these needs, you don't need FIRE. You need to let the rest of us in on the secret! If evaluation demonstrates the presence of some of these needs, start talking about FIRE. Share the idea with singles and families whom you feel would be interested, particularly those whom you would like to see lead. Once the word is out in the parish, make an announcement from the pulpit and put an explanation in the bulletin. Most of the people who join FIRE will do so in response to a personal invitation, but those who don't join will want to feel that they were invited and had the opportunity.

An initial training session for possible leaders will help to spark more interest and more conversation about the program. An initial meeting for all interested people should be held. Advertise well in advance and use local newspapers as well as the church bulletin. FIRE has a special attraction for people who have been away from the church. It seems to offer a safe way back, a place where children can "catch up" on missed sacraments without feeling out of place. An outline for a possible meeting is included at the end of this chapter.

Are The Four Years Of FIRE Sequential? What Happens To A Family That Wants To Join At The Completion Of The First Year?

While there is a theological sequence to the four years of FIRE, it is not necessary for a family to begin with the first year and continue directly through the program. New people can be introduced at the beginning of any of the four years in the cycle. It is, however, valuable to participate from the beginning of each year. The lessons within each year are somewhat dependent on each other, particularly within each liturgical segment. Introducing people mid-year is also often disruptive to a group's developing sense of community.

One solution some parishes have found to introducing people who arrive mid-year is to offer "Creation," the Introductory Segment, each Lent. This gives people a chance to try out the intergenerational learning process, it satisfies those who do not want to wait until the following year to participate, and it offers a parish program for those who may simply be interested in a limited time commitment.

Do The Groups Become Cliques?

Experience has shown that FIRE groups rarely become cliques. The groups tend to develop a strong sense of mission and outreach that forces them beyond themselves into other ministries and communities. Strong leadership plays an important role in this. It is the leader who maintains the connection with the other FIRE groups and challenges members to reach out. Having more than one FIRE group in a parish and offering several opportunities for the groups to come together helps members appreciate themselves as rooted in a larger community.

A related aspect to this problem is the fear that the program as a whole will become elitist. The best way to avoid this problem is to make the initial explanation of FIRE from the altar for everyone, to offer opportunities every year for people to learn about the program and to join groups, to open socials and large group activities to the parish as a whole and to engage in joint activities with the grade-level program and other organizations in the parish.

What Do You Do About Sacramental Preparation?

The single most important thing to say about sacramental preparation is what *not* to do. Do not say that during the sacramental years children must attend "regular" classes. What you are saying to parents when you say this is: "You are capable of sharing faith with your children except when it comes to really important things like sacraments. Then you should send them to us." This will undermine parents' faith in themselves and eventually in the entire program. After all, if FIRE doesn't "work" for the important things, it can't really be teaching the children about God.

If the parish offers special, immediate preparation for the sacraments, (usually four to six weeks, frequently involving parents and children together) FIRE families normally participate in this. These meetings concentrate on the communication of specific knowledge concerning one sacrament. The more general faith knowledge is being taught in the regular grade-level classes or at FIRE meetings. Each year in FIRE contains at least one lesson on Eucharist and one on Reconciliation. Groups should be encouraged to stress these if they have a child who will be receiving one of these sacraments for the first time.

If the entire parish offers no separate immediate preparation for the sacraments, it may be time to consider doing this. FIRE parents are going to want to be involved in this very important time with their children. A specific family preparation could be developed and offered to the parish as a whole as an option.

Confirmation preparation is normally handled simply by involvement in the FIRE program for the number of years the parish requires for Confirmation. The immediate preparation (retreat, special sessions on the Spirit, etc.) needs to be done with the parish as a whole. In the parish where FIRE originated, two workshops a year were also held for Confirmation students in FIRE. The preparation of the Calvary Walk (Year I, Lenten Segment VI) was done by Confirmation students and their sponsors. A workshop on decision-making, also for students and sponsors was usually held in January. Most FIRE students invited members of their small communities to be their sponsors so there was little problem in getting sponsors to attend. Sponsors were also sharing in a very real way in the faith journey of the young people involved simply by participating together with them in FIRE.

FIRE communities will want to be involved in the celebration of the reception of sacraments for their members. They have participated in the faith life of this person. In a very real sense, they are one of the important ways in which the child or young person experiences church. They are an essential part of the church into which the child is being initiated and should be present and involved.

What About Teenagers?

We have teens who participate in FIRE and enjoy it. Usually this works best, though, if they start at an earlier age. Most teens who stay with FIRE say that it is the one place where people listen to them, respect their opinions, and treat them as equals. While I am willing to agree that teens need time with their peers, they spend most of every day with peers, and very little time with adults. The work world into which they are going is intergenerational. FIRE can provide some very worthwhile skills.

Teens also help to keep the rest of us honest and humble. They are a tremendous asset to any FIRE group and should be strongly encouraged to attend.

"Encouraged" is the key word here. Given the freedom to choose, many teenagers will try and like FIRE. On the other hand, nothing is more difficult for a leader, a parent, or a group as a while, than a teen who has been dragged to a meeting. (I speak from experience!)

There are probably as many different questions as there are people and parishes who will use FIRE. FIRE, as you have already found out, is much more interested in helping people to discover their own questions, than it is in providing answers.

With that in mind, please treat all these "answers" as general guidelines, not rules. You know the people of your own community; you know their needs. Meet with them; pray, plan, and play with them. Together you will be able to decide what will work best for your parish.

An Introductory Meeting

Materials: blocks, scrap paper and pencils, a large writing surface such as a blackboard for feedback, nametags, a table, Bible, registration forms.

1. As people enter for the meeting, greet them at the door, gently hand them a plain building block, and ask them to put on a name tag.

2. Begin with a simple opening song.

3. Explain that the evening is going to demonstrate how FIRE works as well as explain about the program.

4. Invite everyone to build something alone with their block. Ask for volunteers to explain what they have built. Then ask people to build something with the person next to them or the people in their row. Finally (if the group is not too large) invite everyone to come forward and make something all together. Don't be surprised if people are a little hesitant about playing and don't get concerned.

5. Wait for everyone to be seated and to quiet down. Read 1 Peter 2:4-6 very quietly.

6. Explain that we are all living "blocks." Alone we can't be built into much. In a small group, we can be more, but all together, look at the beautiful building we can make. This is the whole point of church. Each of us is given a gift for building up the community. FIRE is going to help us to see and use that gift.

7. Now ask everyone to use their imaginations. The pope and the world council of churches are terribly upset about the condition of the church in the world. A group of you are being sent to live on an island for thirty years and to re-organize the church. To do this, you can bring two books with you, and three articles. In thirty years you will be asked to return and bring the church back to the rest of the world.

8. What will your church look like? Will you meet at all? How will you determine leadership? What kind of celebrations will you have? What things will be important to you? How will you teach the children? What will you believe in? Is there anything your church will feel called upon to do for the

rest of the world? (You may find it helpful to have these questions written out for each group or mounted visibly.)

9. Break into groups of five or six. Allow twenty minutes for discussion. Put one of your new leaders in each group to keep the discussion on track.

10. After twenty minutes, bring the groups back and put the feedback on the board. If you allow the groups to go longer than that, they are apt to get bogged down in unimportant points. It is also important not to let them get bogged down in the articles they are going to bring; these are simply discussion starters.

11. Most groups create a church that is a community, that prays, celebrates, and learns together, that reaches out to others. This is the church of the New Testament, the church of the Spirit that is engraved in all our hearts. FIRE is modeled after this church and looks very much like it.

12. Explain that every time we do religious education we are creating the church thirty years from now. If this is the church that we want, then our religious education should model that church. That is the whole point of FIRE: to provide an experience of church while modeling what we want to work at and hope to become.

13. Explain briefly the educational philosophy of FIRE and the way in which a FIRE meeting is conducted. Discuss the particular role it will have in your parish and how sacraments will be handled. Take a few moments to explain intergenerational learning. FIRE isn't adults teaching children. It is adults and children learning, praying and playing together.

14. Take time to answer any questions. Inform the group when your "planning committee" will be meeting and invite them to attend.

15. Pass out registration forms and pencils. Stress the fact that you will need the name of every person in the family who will be participating and each child's age.

16. Close with a song and refreshments.

This is simply a suggestion. You may desire to introduce your parish in a totally different manner. You know your community best.

6

Conclusion

"...Would you please tell me which way I ought to go from here?"

"That depends a good deal on where you want to get to," said the cat.

"I don't much care where," said Alice.

"Then it doesn't matter which way you go," said the cat.

"...so long as I get somewhere," Alice added as an explanation.

"Oh, you're sure to do that," said the cat, "If you only walk long enough."[1]

The age of Christendom is ended. The symbiosis of the Judeo-Christian ethic and society that long outlived the

Reformation has finally disintegrated. With it, the present model of religious education has died. Tom Walters' national survey on directors and coordinators of religious education, Andrew Greeley's numerous studies on the faith of U.S. Catholics, the Gallup Polls, the Hartford study by Hector La-Chappelle at Hartford Seminary have all certified that it is dead. The brain wave is flat, the spirit is gone, yet we refuse to bury it. We continue to spend millions of dollars on life-support systems to keep a dead heart beating, a dead body breathing. We are afraid to let go. Even a dead body is better than the abyss of nothingness we would face if we did let go.

We are confused by the changing lifestyles of the American family and the changing position of the church in society. We are overwhelmed by the increasing demands placed on religious education to prepare Christians who are knowledge-able, moral, and faith-filled. We are devastated by its rapidly escalating failure rate. We do not know which direction to take; we do not know where we are going or where we should go. And so we have convinced ourselves that as long as we keep walking, we are bound to get somewhere.

FIRE is not the answer to all religious education's problems. FIRE is the hope that an answer is possible. FIRE is the spark to encourage others to sit down in the ever-in-creasing darkness and decide where it is we are going and what new directions we must take to get there. But first, we must stop walking!

It is an awesome thing to begin.

Note

1. Lewis Carroll. *The Adventures of Alice in Wonderland.* (New York: Clarkson N. Potter, 1973) p. 55.

Selected Bibliography

Albright, William F. *The Biblical Period from Abraham to Ezra.* New York: Harper and Row, 1963.

Anderson, Bernhard W. *Understanding the Old Testament.* Englewood Cliffs, N.J.: Prentice Hall, 1975.

Aquinas, Thomas. *Summa Theologica.* Chicago: Encyclopedia Brittanica, 1952.

Avila, Rafael. *Worship and Politics.* Maryknoll, N.Y.: Orbis, 1981.

Bausch, William. *A New Look at the Sacraments.* W. Mystic: Twenty-Third Publications, 1977.

Benson, J. and Hilyard, J. *Becoming a Family.* Collegeville: St. Mary's Press, 1978.

Berger, Peter. *The Noise of Solemn Assemblies.* Garden City: Doubleday, 1961.

_____. *Rumor of Angels.* Garden City: Doubleday, 1969.

Brown, Raymond E. *Crises Facing the Church.* New York: Paulist, 1975.

_____. *Jesus, God and Man.* New York: Macmillan, 1973.

_____. *The Virginal Conception and Bodily Resurrection of Jesus.* New York: Paulist, 1973.

Brueggemann, Walter. *The Prophetic Imagination.* Philadelphia: Fortress Press, 1978.

Carroll, Lewis. *Alice's Adventures in Wonderland.* New York: Clarkson N. Potter, Inc., 1973.

Chance, Paul. "Master of Mastery," *Psychology Today,* April 1987, pp. 42-48.

Chesto, Kathleen. "Creating Ear Plays from Scripture," *The Catechist,* April, 1982.

Curran, Dolores. *In the Beginning There Were Parents.* Minneapolis: Winston, 1978.

_____. and DeGidio, O.S.M., Sandra. *Family: A Catechetical Challenge for the 80s.* Washington: U.S.C.C., 1979.

DeGidio, O.S.M., Sandra. *Sharing Faith in the Family.* W. Mystic: Twenty-Third Publications, 1980.

DeMello, Anthony. *Song of the Bird.* Chicago: Loyola University Press, 1982.

DeVaux, Roland. *The Early History of Israel.* Philadelphia: Westminster Press, 1978.

Doohan, Leonard. *The Lay-Centered Church.* Minneapolis: Winston, 1984.

Dufresne, Edward R. *Partnership: Marriage and the Committed Life.* New York: Paulist, 1975.

Dulles, S.J., Avery. *Models of Revelation.* Garden City: Doubleday, 1985.

Ellis, C.SS.R., Peter. *The Men and the Message of the Old Testament.* Collegeville: Liturgical Press, 1976.

Fenhagen, James. *Mutual Ministry.* New York: Seabury, 1977.

Fischer, Kathleen R. *The Inner Rainbow: Imagination in Christian Life.* Ramsey, N.J.: Paulist, 1983.

Fowler, James. *Stages of Faith.* San Francisco: Harper and Row, 1981.

Gallagher, S.J., Chuck. *Evenings for Parents.* New York: W.H. Sadlier, 1976.

Groome, Thomas. *Christian Religious Education.* San Francisco: Harper and Row, 1980.

Guzie, Tad. *The Book of Sacramental Basics.* New York: Paulist, 1981.

_____. *Jesus and the Eucharist.* New York: Paulist, 1974.

Hall, Brian. *Shepherds and Lovers: A Guide to Spiritual Leadership in Christian Ministry.* New York: Paulist, 1982.

Harris, Maria, ed. *Parish Religious Education.* New York: Paulist, 1978.

Holt, John. *How Children Fail.* New York: Pitman Publishing Corporation, 1964.

Jerome Biblical Commentary. Englewood Cliffs, N.J.: Prentice Hall Publishers, 1968.

Jerusalem Bible. Garden City: Doubleday, 1966.

Kerns, S.J. Joseph E. *The Theology of Marriage.* New York: Sheed & Ward, 1964.

Kung, Hans. *The Church.* Garden City: Doubleday, 1967.

Leary, James E. *Hear, O Israel.* Waldwick, N.J.: Arena Letters, 1980.

Merton, Thomas. *Contemplative Prayer.* Garden City: Doubleday, 1971.

Miller, Donald E., Snyder, Gradon F. and Neff, Robert W. *Using Biblical Simulations.* Valley Forge: Judson Press, 1980.

Mitchell, Leonel L. *The Meaning of Ritual.* Ramsey: Paulist, 1977.

Moran, Gabriel. *Design for Religion.* New York: Seabury, 1971.

_____. *The Present Revelation: In Quest of Religious Foundations.* New York: Seabury, 1972.

_____. *Theology of Revelation.* New York: Seabury, 1966.

_____. *Vision and Tactics: Toward an Adult Church.* New York: Seabury, 1968.

New American Bible. New York: Benziger, Inc., 1970.

Neibuhr, H. Richard. *Christ and Culture.* New York: Harper and Row, 1951.

Nouwen, Henri. *Creative Ministry.* Garden City: Doubleday, 1978.

Padovano, Anthony. *Who Is Christ.* Notre Dame: Ave Maria Press, 1974.

Paul VI. "On Evangelization in the Modern World," 8 December 1975.

Sawin, Margaret. *Family Enrichment with Family Clusters.* Valley Forge: Judson Press, 1979.

_____. *Hope for Families.* New York: Sadlier, 1982.

Schillebeeckx, Edward. *Jesus: An Experiment in Christology.* Translated by Hubert Hoskins. New York: Seabury, 1979.

Shea, John. *Stories of Faith.* Chicago: Thomas More Press, 1980.

Strong, James E. *Exhaustive Concordance of the Bible.* New York: Abingdon Press, 1963.

Tugwell, Simon. *The Beatitudes: Soundings in Christian Spirituality.* Springfield: Templegate Publishers, 1980.

United States Catholic Conference. "Sharing the Light of Faith," *National Catechetical Directory.* 17 November 1977.

Vatican Council II. "The Constitution on the Sacred Liturgy," *Sacrosanctum concilium,* 4 December 1963.

_____. "Dogmatic Constitution on the Church," *Lumen gentium,* 21 November 1964.

_____. "Decree on the Apostolate of Lay People," *Apostolicam Actvositatem,* 18 November 1965.

_____. "Pastoral Constitution on the Church in the Modern World," *Gaudium et spes,* 7 December 1965.

Vatican Synod Secretariat. "The Role of the Family in the Modern World," 19 July 1979.

Vawter, Bruce. *This Man Jesus.* New York: Doubleday, 1975.

VonRad, Gerhard. *Old Testament Theology.* New York: Harper and Row, 1962.

Westerhoff, III, John A. *Will Our Children Have Faith?* New York: Seabury, 1976.

_____. and Neville, Gwen Kennedy. *Learning through Liturgy.* New York: Seabury, 1978.

Wright, G. Ernest. *Biblical Archeology.* Philadelphia: Westminster Press, 1960.

Appendix A

Evaluation for Group Members

1. How did you hear about FIRE?

2. Why did you become involved in the program?

3. Do you feel that your group is becoming (has become) a community to whom you could turn for support? What has helped or hindered this process?

4. Did you read Scripture before becoming involved in this program? Have those reading habits changed in any way?

*5. Do you talk about God more as a family since joining FIRE?

*6. Would you say that FIRE has

a. assisted you in handing on your values to your children?

b. challenged your values?

c. both?

d. neither?

*7. Is FIRE an alternative to the children's religious education program in your parish or a supplement? How do you feel about that?

8. Has this program challenged or encouraged you to become involved in ministry? In social justice issues? Be specific.

9. What do you see as the specific strengths of this program?

10. What are its greatest weaknesses?

11. Choose one FIRE Lesson that you (your family) especially enjoyed. Why was the experience enjoyable? What do you feel you learned from it?

*These questions are to be answered only by families with children.

Appendix B

Evaluation for Administrators

1. Was the FIRE program done in your church or presented in your family ministry curriculum as

   a. an enrichment program?

   b. an alternative to existing Christian education programs?

   c. a family retreat experience?

2. What specific needs did you hope to meet by doing this program?

3. How were your leaders trained?

   a. a full day training workshop

   b. ongoing leader meetings with prayer and theological input

   c. they were not trained

4. Was the training sufficient? Please comment.

5. Please describe the composition of your group(s)

   ____number of two parent families with children

   ____number of one parent families with children

   ____number of single or married adults without children

6. Do you feel that the group(s) grew together as a community? What helped or hindered the process?

7. What do you see as the specific strengths of this program?

8. What do you feel are its greatest weaknesses?

9. Has this program impacted your church as a whole in any way?